COSTUME REVOLUTION

COSTUME REVOLUTION

Textiles, clothing and costume of the Soviet Union in the Twenties.

by Lidya Zaletova, Fabio Ciofi degli Atti, Franco Panzini, and others.
Translated by Elizabeth Dafinone

Trefoil Publications, London

First published with the collaboration of the GFT Group
by CATALOGHI MARSILIO, Venice, for the exhibition *L'Abito della Rivoluzione*

Organizing Committee: T. Strizenova E. Karavaeva L. Aksenova O. Vlasova O. Zemljakova E. Ivanova E. Mylnikova A. Smirina T. Fomiceva Marta Alessandri John Bowlt Fabio Ciofi degli Atti Massimo Dolcini Nicoletta Misler Franco Panzini
Graphics Massimo Dolcini Carlo Becatti
Photography V. Estigneev V. Sokolov

First English language edition 1989 by Trefoil Publications Ltd, London

British Library Cataloguing in Publication Data

ISBN 0-86294-175-X

Strizenova, Tatiana
    Costume revolution
    1. Soviet costume, 1917-1953
    I. Title
    391'.00947

Typeset by Titus Wilson Ltd
Printed by Graphicom, Vicenza, Italy.
US copyright & title pages

CONTENTS

FOREWORD TO THE ORIGINAL EDITION

Like culture, clothing is primarily a means of expression, which reflects a social reality in which the individual communicates social needs, aspects and specific roles. So, when the proposal was put to us of realising, for the first time in Italy, the exhibition on Soviet Constructivism which has inspired this book, we immediately found the idea fascinating.

Specifically, what stimulated us most about this project was the possibility it presented of highlighting the cultural components of clothing, and the innovative role that the sector has always played from the social point of view.

The historical period in which *Costume Revolution* is set, that is the period which followed the 1917 revolution in the Soviet Union, is from this point of view a particularly interesting period. In an atmosphere of such a marked evolutionary process, that of revolution, what emerged particularly was the strict inter-relation between social processes and innovative processes in taste, which we find in the exhibits and which reflect the rapport between art and industry.

Now that the initial objective has been fulfilled, I want to thank the firms who collaborated in order to make all this possible. In the first place the USSR Ministry of Culture, who allowed the GFT Group to play an active role in the creation of the organizational structure, and also the Italian-USSR Association and the people of Pesaro, Florence and Piedmont. Lastly an enormous thanks to the organizing committee – in particular to Lidya Zaletova, Fabio Ciofi degli Atti, and Franco Panzini – for the valuable, penetrating and substantial amount of work involved.

Marco Rivetti *President and Managing Director, GFT Group*

INTRODUCTORY ESSAYS

TEXTILES AND SOVIET FASHION IN THE TWENTIES

Tatyana Strizenova

The October revolution of 1917 was a watershed between the old and the new, revolutionary art. The development of a new society, based on the paramount role of the worker, brought about a change in the social role of art. Slogans such as 'Art for the people' and 'Art for industry', born of the masses, together with Lenin's propaganda programme, reflected the fundamental objectives of the time. The first areas of artistic production to be overrun by this radical innovative process were those directly linked to daily life, such as furniture, fabrics, clothes and crockery. The possibility of producing these things industrially was at the origin of the theory of productivity, helping to form the new man and changing the concrete reality in which he found himself. However the slogan 'Art for industry' did not find practical application on a large scale in the Twenties; the young Soviet State, having just recovered from a tragic civil war, was more concerned to instigate economic reconstruction.

The main results achieved by the pioneers of productivity were epitomized primarily in textiles and clothing design, in the development of a modern taste, particularly in fabrics, and in the widespread appearance of novel geometric and thematic designs. At the same time costume design geared itself towards the creation of a comfortable and functional dress for the populace.

FABRICS

The first measure taken by the Soviet government in the textile sector was the establishment of a Textile Workers Union. This aimed at the reorganization of the entire sector with the use of a network based on trust, into which the traditional centers of the Russian textile industry, Moscow, Petrograd, Ivanovo- Voznesensk, Tver and others could come together.

The revolutionary spirit was expressed in fabric production by original and distinct characteristics. With the exception of trimmings, traditional flowers and foliage were no longer allowed to dominate, nor was it acceptable for the fabric designer to be considered as a simple artisan.

It should be remembered that at the beginning of the Twenties, the country was falling into economic difficulties caused by the civil war, and consequently many manufacturers were inactive due to a lack of primary materials, energy sources and labour. Simplicity of materials and of design, therefore, characterized the few fabrics produced.

Manufacturers found themselves faced with immense problems, not only in re-establishing the industry, but also in eradicating the traditional role of the textile artist, and in totally overhauling design, thereby abandoning orthodoxy for the unknown, and restating the creative value of that form of art.

Around 1923 the situation of the textile industry stabilized, and it became possible for many manufacturers throughout Russia, including, amongst others, Aleksandra Exter, the Sternberg brothers and El Lissitsky, to participate in the Artistic-Industrial Exhibition. In the same year *Pravda* published an appeal for artists to go and work in the factories in order to revive fabric design. Two noted painters, Liubov Popova and Varvara Stepanova, responded immediately and went to run the design workshop First Factory of Printed Cotton in Moscow. These artists considered their laborious new work far more important and significant than easel painting; this pure art had the power to realize the romantic ideal of a marriage between art and modern industry and allowed for a total aesthetic transformation of life.

Popova and Stepanova both belonged to the group of Constructivist artists associated with the *Lef* journal, founded by Vladimir Tatlin, Alexandra Rodchenko, Aleksandra Exter, the Sternberg brothers and El Lissitsky, whose ideological works coincided in many ways with the theory of productivity. A lot of their early theories and methods of designing useful functional objects lost their over-elaborate style and were incorporated into the Vkutemas' syllabus in 1921.

It is illuminating that Bauhaus' programme (founded at Weimar by Walter Gropius in 1919) differed little in its substance from the ideas of this group of Soviet designers. From Bauhaus' design laboratories, studios and workshops, emerged furniture, lamps and fabrics of a completely new type; and at this point, it is important to emphasize that this style of design eventually brought about the transformation of the industrial assembly line. Naturally, links between the Soviet producers and Bauhaus resulted.

In 1924 Stepanova clearly defined this style of new decorative fabrics in a brief report issued by

V. Stepanova with stage fittings from 'The Death of Tarelkin' by A. Suchovo-Kobylin produced by V. Meyerhold, 1922.

the INKHUK (Institute of Artistic Culture) entitled the 'Struggle against organized design: for a geometric design of shapes'. Circles, cylinders, criss-crosses and zigzags melted into one another, and at other times were unexpectedly juxtaposed. Often patterns were cribbed from industrial reality, and cogs, wheels, and levers were portrayed. The symbols of the new Soviet state, the hammer and sickle and the red star were also used.

Not all Popova and Stepanova's designs – considered in textile reproduction as bichromatic – are of equal merit. Some adapt readily to the material, harmonizing with the structural characteristics of the cotton, whilst others have more prominent outlines and appear heavy and dull on the indienne cotton. Both the artists had previously dedicated themselves to theatrical costume, and therefore understood the importance of the links between design and shape. Influenced by the Cubist movement they reproduced similar styles in textiles so that, compared to the life-less and anonymous production of that time, their works constantly surprised with their audacious, novel designs and lively colours. It was these elements which determined their extraordinary success, to the point where one can speak of their creations as the being the 'first Soviet fashion'. The press at that time wrote: 'The marquisette' and indienne have not only become refined but have risen to the level of an extraordinary art in a period just as extraordinary; the intense colours and vibrant artistic decorations flow like interminable rivers through cities right across the frontiers of our immense Republic'[1].

At the same time as Stepanova and Popova, many notable painters, sculptors and architects competed with fabric designs. Among them we remember Konstantin Juon, Alexander Vesnin, Vera Muchina, Aleksandra Exter, Sergei Cechonin, but for the most part their designs unfortunately, remain unknown to us. If there is any doubt that the geometries of Stepanova and Popova greatly influenced the textile industry in the Twenties, there is no doubt whatsoever that only a small number of artists, mainly painters, were enticed by the abstract Constructivist view: the trend that became predominant at that time followed a different path. The wish to actively take part in the construction of a new life, demanded a more concrete language, the presence of a subject, albeit different from the traditional one, and a close link with the contemporary problems. Thus a new type of thematic and also propagandist (*agitaciony*) design was born, which included, among the more general topics, subjects such as industrialization, dockyards, factories, aeroplanes, sport, pioneers, the new reality of the countryside, the Budennyj cavalry, etc. Artistic impressions of these topics were used as unusual propaganda instruments. The way in which impromptu fabrics became fashionable within a ten year span, is a complex and extremely heterogeneous phenomenon, which lends itself to lively discussion but it also presents original and easily identifiable themes. The same is also applicable to the activity of a large group of interesting artists such as Sergei Burylin, Maria Nazarevskaja, Olga Bogoslovskaja, Mikhail Chvostenko, Darya Preobrazenskaja and many others whose names remain obscure, but whose fabrics are preserved in the archives of textile factories, museums and private collections.

In the thematic textile designs of the Twenties we can see a dual pattern of interpretation of the subject: one, following the traditional style of easel painting and the other a purely abstract geometrization. One of the pioneers of this second tendency was Oskar Grjun, designer at the Trechgornaja Manuaktura. It was Grjun who created one of the most noted and highly expressive works of the early Twenties: the emblems of the Soviet State, the design of which he drastically and originally revised. With the ear of corn, the hammer and sickle depicted against the background of a circular band (a stylization of the suns rays), and the red foreground scattered with golden stars, he typified the romantic halo that shone over the Soviet country. Thanks also to the intense colour associations of scarlet, gold and cherry red, the artist succeeded in cramming an extraordinary decorative vigour into the significance of that image. The design was presented at the Paris Exhibition of Decorative Arts in 1925. In interpreting the subject, Grjun's work is quite unique. The decorative idea, more widespread in the Twenties, is in fact an image which links almost mechanically the old ornate floral designs with the new themes. Another notable artist, also from Ivanovo, is V. Masloc, who made shiny and gaudy satins and indiennes

Photograph of L. Mayakovsky with pupils in the Fifties.

and whose compositions were based on the inter-
lacing of luxuriant garlands of flowers. Inserted in
these little picture frames and trompe l'oeil was
the new reality of the countryside where technology was replacing manual labour. For example,
in the fabric 'The new reality of the countryside'
all the figurative components were outlined with
the minutest of care and patience. The individual
varieties of flowers in the garlands made unique
frames for the pictures which depicted work
scenes, the countryside itself and the landscape in
which spatial depth was realized and emphasized
by clouds wandering in the sky. What is favoured
in Maslov's work is the ingenious way of offsetting
a traditional composition, returning to the old
ornamental silk fabrics, with the new style of
depicting a theme inserted within.

Perhaps the artist specifically made these
designs, which required a considerable amount of
work, for the exhibition *Bytovoj Sovetskij tekstil*
(Soviet textiles in daily life) which took place in
1928. The compositions by Maslov were unique.
The great majority of artists had in fact a preference
for one type of symbolic design in which the subject was inserted inside a conventional geometric
structure based on modular scanning. These original decorative themes were really a typical
expression of their time and provided the basis
for such exhibitions as *Bytovoj Sovetskoe tekstil*
(Soviet textiles in daily life) and later on, between
1931-32, *Sovetskoe promyslennoe iskusstvo* (Soviet
industrial art).

The more widespread fabric series had simple
designs, based on the repetition of a single symbolic unit, stylized and drawn in mathematical
terms to the extent that detail was totally ironed
out and yet still recognizable, whilst at other times
the accent was placed on one single but highly
expressive aspect.

It was these designs that were favoured by
Grjun. His *Spools* and *Pioneers* indiennes distinguished themselves with their graceful and delicate colouring. The figure of the pioneer with
the red bandana, for example – depicted quite
precisely – is very clear, whilst the row of upright
little figures on the intense red surface of the fabric
gives the impression of a rhythmic design on the
march.

These designs appeared particularly lively on
lightweight cotton fabrics such as indienne, marquisette, crepe, armure and voile, which were

fashionable in the Twenties. Now and again the
subject was made up of letters or interrelated words
hidden inside an ingenious design, a kind of puzzle
difficult to decipher: *KIM* (Youth International),
15 years of the USSR, 18 March, Don and others.

A notable place among the design themes was
held by fabrics made for children. From these we
remember above all others the works of Ivanovo
Olga Bogoslovskaja, *Drums, The crocket, Little
hammers*. The rhythm of the composition and the
diagonal compilation of the theme create a dynamic
but balanced impression.

By contrast geometric lines and serious themes
are the characteristic traits of the textiles that we
have defined as 'propagandist' (*agittekstil*). To
some extent these fabrics were influenced by Stepanova and Popova's style and are therefore Constructivist. Nevertheless the firm beliefs of
exponents of the general *agittekstil* induced them
to characterize it as a genre and a style of representation rather than Constructivism, as it were a sort
of narration by painting.

The limited technological facilities and the lack
of a wide range of dyes were the cause of the
chromatic poverty of these textiles; but, despite
having no more than two to three colours at his
disposal, the artist often managed to achieve an
extraordinary intensity and decorative effect. Take
for example a work by the painter Liubov Silic,
The reapers, done for her degree thesis. Inspired by
the old *Picot*, the artist created a refined, delicately
outlined design, using only two colours, blue and
white. The example of Sergei Burylin from
Ivanovo is also unique. Without having had any
specific tuition he achieved the utmost profession-
alism in his work. Compositional skill and virtu-
oso command of design distinguished indiennes
such as *Industry, Tractors, Ships* and others. One
of the merits of these manufactured articles lies in
the dynamism of the composition and in the ability
with which movement is realized, in such a way
that tractors, ships and locomotives do really seem
to be moving on the surface of the material. The
clarity of movement in these designs is interesting
not only because of their widespread variety but
because a symbol of the new era emerges, representing the frantic way ahead towards a new
creation of the young Soviet nation.

A large group of textiles with thematic designs
depict figurative themes and compositions of

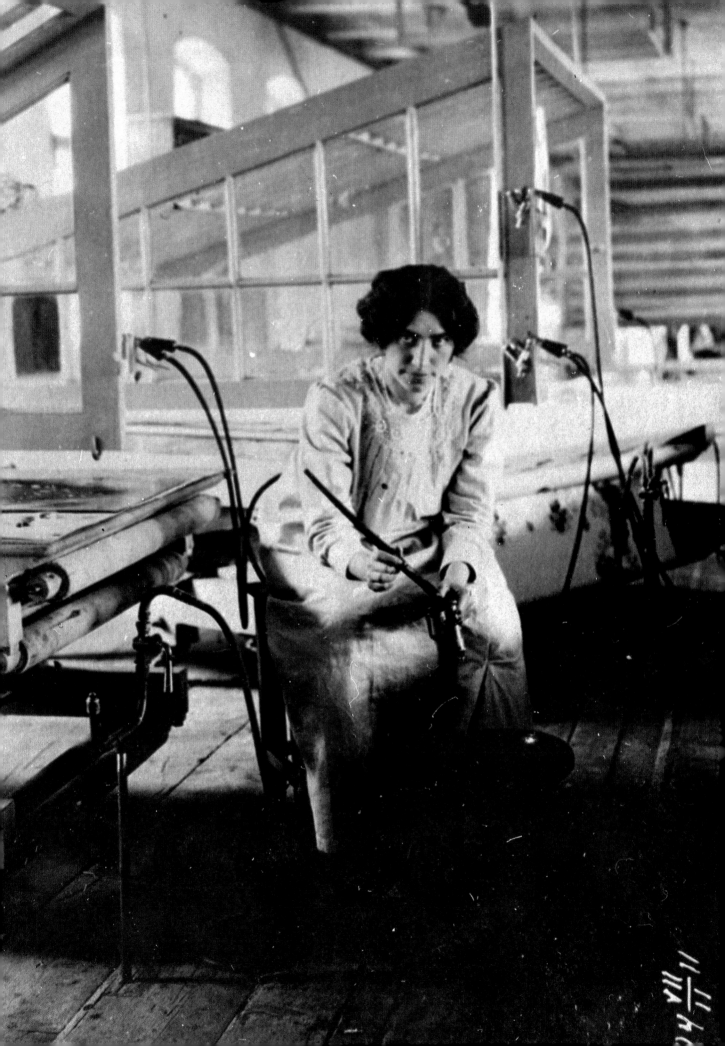

notable complexity: the heraldic structure and the totally imagined but conventionally coded characters call for a serious degree of concentration by the observer, in order to understand the sense. In most of these designs, the artist achieves notable decorative effects and reveals great professional skill. This sign-language forces him to choose ingenious techniques of great semantic importance, which also reveal their significance through the symbolism of colours.

In the depiction of commemorative parades, sporting competitions or industrial life, artists such as Maria Naarevskaja, Darija Preobrazenskaja, Pavel Leonov, Raisa Matveeva, Maria Anufrieva, reveal a notable originality and achieve great intensity in the interpretation of aspects of contemporary life. Of great importance in the development of textile design in the Twenties was the work of Ludmilla Mayakowsky, sister of the poet Vladimir Mayakovsky, who is credited with having perfected the spray-gun technique for fabrics.

For many years Mayakovsky worked with her spray-guns, firstly at the *Troochgornaja Manufaktura* and then in the *Krasnaja Roza* factory. Her geometric designs reflected Suprematism and Cubism, giving them the characteristics of an as yet unknown Constructivism, but these designs also possessed softened tones, delicate and fluid circular lines, angular figures, and shells, without giving way to an explicit animism germinated by the merging of geometric shapes. An extraordinary pictorial quality was made possible thanks to the use of velvet material favoured by Mayjakovsky in her experiments.

This book presents the works of an artist as yet fairly unknown, Natalya Kiseleva, whose textiles appeared for the most part at the end of the Twenties, and which were produced by the factory *Krasnaja Roza*. In these manufactured fabrics geometric and pictorial qualities were reunited. At times it was a question of multi-coloured fabrics, at other times, it was fabrics that made use of shades of one colour, but in both cases the chromatic characteristics of the design were determined by fading sequences of related undertones. It is this that gives Kiseleva's fabrics their pictorial softness and lustre, an effect also achieved by the use of the spray-gun, a technique that the artist had learnt and mastered from Mayakovsky.

Some types of design were put into light-hearted categories. The inhabitants of Central Asia, for example, favoured lively satins and this series of fabrics was named *Life and costumes of Oriental people*. In managing to adapt techniques to the traditional Central Asian fabrics like indiennes and satins, the thematic designs gained great popularity, for example *Turksib* (a symbol that was to indicate the construction of the Turkish-Siberian line) and *Likbez* (for the 'Liquidation of illiteracy').

In the range of thematic designs we see a great disparity of styles and results. The boldest supporters of *agittekstil* decidedly rejected traditional painting and the fundamental problems of the propriety of the support-fabric, in order to allow themselves instead to be wholly led by the objective of portraying reality in a more faithful way. However they did not analyze their own decorations, but using the word 'rapport', they preferred to define their work by adopting, in open contradiction, the artistic terms for easel painting. The extreme difficulty in taking sides, the frequent commercial art representation of rapport, and above all the frontal and pictorial solution of a contemporary theme, all provoked violent discussion and argument in the press, while in the meantime, the artists' interest in subject themes was gradually fading. Whilst elucidating the role of the *agittekstil* in the history of textiles, its enormous positive significance was as a first step towards a greatly creative and less craft-orientated approach to industrial design: this should not be under-valued. Amid the innumerable discussions which surround the 'meaning' of textiles this type of design must have a serious bearing on the specific qualities of its language and possibilities.

At the beginning of the Thirties many design workshops were created inside factories and in 1930 the Moscow Textile Institute was founded. Turning fashion around, floral designs replaced the thematic subject, but were based on themes from living nature: shapes from the world of vegetables, flowers, foliage, plants, branches, were triumphant up until the end of the Thirties.

The works of best designers distinguished themselves with their freshness in reproducing natural shapes and in the pertinence of the design to the material's structure. For example, in the indiennes of the Ivanovo artist V. Gurkovskaja, we find elemental and minuscule designs – sprigs of rye, camomile and cornflowers vanish into a smooth dark background, and at times little sheets of paper are sketched in a graphic style – this type of design together with dots and rings totally dominate the first half of the Thirties.

The production of silks, basically in *crepe de Chine* was highlighted by the *Krasnaja Roza* factory in Moscow, where more conventional floral themes predominated: poppies, carnations and jasmine. The possibilities disclosed by the new technique of photographic printing brought about a reflection on the efficiency of colour handling and a correlation between smooth backgrounds and pale designs. Ingenious works by artists such as V. Skljarova, V. Lotonina, S. Agajan and others are still used today: shown in pictorial patterns, they pair up lightly and delicately in their discrete simplicity, overcoming for harmony chromatic mixing. During these years, the manufacturing groups created the concept of personal style'which spread into the special language of textile design. From this moment the fabric designer ceased to be anonymous.

FASHION

Immediately after the October revolution, as in many other sectors of the national economy, the restructuring of the clothing industry began. Around 1921 many dressmakers and tailors stopped working independently and came under the control of the State. Furthermore, although textile factories were in a position to produce limited quantities of a few types of fabrics, these were of poor quality due to the country's difficult economic situation and were mainly military cloth, canvas, sack cloth and indienne.

A great many people were dressed poorly and many still wore old pre-revolutionary clothes. Military dress became more widespread: leather jackets made out of tanned hides, military tunics and uniforms. The Red Army uniform became the first example of the new type of garment when in 1918, the painter Boris Kustodev won a competition to design the army headdress and overcoat. The choice of design was dictated by the romantic spirit of the revolutionary era: in fact the creator revived old historic Russia, replicating the Russian

army helmet worn at the battle of Kulikovo, and basing the design of the overcoat on the caftan. In this way the famous *Budenovka* with the red star and the grey overcoat with scarlet lapels and superimposed tabs called *Razgovory* was born. The colour red, symbol of the revolution, was the principal decorative element of the uniform.

Great significance was attributed to the creation of new forms of clothes for the workers. In 1918, in the complicated situation of civil war and on the initiative of the famous stylist Nadezda Lamanova, taken up by the People's Commission for Education, the Workshop of Contemporary Dress was set up. Its aims were formulated by Lamanova herself at the first *All-Russian Conference of Art and Industry* in 1919. 'Art must penetrate all walks of daily life, stimulating the artistic taste and sensitivity of the masses. Artists in the field of dress, using basic materials, must create simple but at the same time beautiful clothes that are suited to the new demands of working life'[2]. Because of the economic crisis, the formulations of Lamanova might have remained a mere theoretical show', but in the Twenties a large group of designers – Alexandra Exter, Ljubov Popova, Alexander Rodchenko, the Vesnin brothers and others – started experimenting to create new forms of clothing that were functional, simple, comfortable and adaptable to both living and working conditions.

The famous stylist Nedezda Lamanova, an example of sincere dedication to the revolutionary cause and the ideals of the new society was, in 1917, at the age of 56, already a prestigious couturier and owner of a fashion house with an exclusive clientele, yet she condoned, without hesitation, the revolution. In confirmation of this, she writes in her autobiography 'To make functional and beautiful clothing is a sign of making life more comfortable and beautiful, not only for privilieged people but also for a large strata of the population. That has always been my conviction . . . . The Revolution has altered my economic condition, but has not changed my ideas on life, in fact it has given me the possibility of realising them in a infinitely wider context.'[3]

Lamanova had at her disposal the simple and economic materials of those years, flimsy textiles, with dull shades, badly dyed and of limited width: military cloth, canvas, indienne and fustian. With an almost architectural approach the stylist aimed at a practical cut and a clear line, with simplicity and clarity in the proportions. The popular costume obsessed her, so it was therefore natural for Lamanova to aspire to it. What appealed to her about popular costume was the traditional rectangular shape: many of her models are, in fact, fantastic variations of the rectangule, translated into blouses, cassocks, shirts, jackets including the caftans mentioned above which were worn as overalls. The choice of the rectangle shape was also determined by the caracteristics of the material used, a statement that today may seem elementary, but which was in those days a real discovery of Lamanova's. The smooth materials and the simple cut lent themselves to decorative elements, embroidery and borders characteristic of popular costume. The use of trimmings was however limited to elegant clothes. Their clean cut and simplicity made Lamanova's models easy to mass-produce, a quality to which the creator attached great importance. It was not by chance that The Workshop of Contemporary Dress was awarded a prize at the general All-Russian Exhibition of Applied Industrial Art. The silhouette and the elongated proportions of Lamanova's clothes were not very different from European trends in fashion but they distinguished themselves above all by one particular detail, a severe purity, and thanks to the grace with which they were inspired by national costume in the cut and decorative elements, they also won the Grand Prix at the Paris Exhibition of Decorative Arts in 1925. Afterwards Lamanova kept in close contact with the famous French couturier Poiret and every year spent long periods in Paris. Finally, Lamanova was mentioned in the manifesto of Soviet fashion published in 1928, which may be summarised in the following phrase: 'Why, for whom and of what is costume made? It is all summed up in its form'[4].

Alongside Lamanova we should remembered Alexandra Exter, an major protagonist of Soviet fashion in the Twenties. Exter had started her artistic career as a painter, scenographer, and theatrical costumer, but the general movement towards making functional and useful objects steered her towards clothing. In wanting useful and simple forms, Exter is undoubtedly close to Lamanova, and despite her tendency to create a type of clothing which had a limited circulation, her so-called 'work overall' (*prozodezda*), affirms the necessity for clothing to be differentiated, according to the particular job that the wearer is doing. In this sense her position was directly opposed to that of the supporters of a unitary work dress. Exter paid particular attention to the aesthetic qualities of practical clothing, its chromatic rhythm, the suitability of different types of material and the complex harmony of its proportions. Her sketches show various designs based on simple geometric forms: rectangles, circles and triangles within which a decorative or geometrical motif was often inserted, and which was reminiscent of her Cubist style painting. However, the geometry of the designs was linked to the simplicity of the cut and her clear awareness for the need for mass-produced clothes. In 1923 Exter wrote in the periodical *Atel'e*: 'the problem of a new style is the order of the day . . . From the moment that our working classes represented the vast majority of the population, clothes had to be adapted to the workers and in particular to the type of activity that they are engaged in'[5]. Her style changed therefore into the creation of so-called 'individual' dress: here Exter gave in to practicality and simplicity; but on the other hand the form was split into single geometric sections; in a single costume structurally different materials were brought together in an elaborate colourful ensemble. Often it is clear that she attempted to mix interchangeable sections together until stratified models comparable to theatrical costumes were achieved with great emotive force and a lively, expressive, nonchalance.

In sketching the clothes the stylist did not worry particularly about measuring the cut millimetre by millimetre, but tended to produce an anonymous work of art, thereby fulfilling the promise for a new type of fashion creation. A great contribution to the projection of the new type of dress was given by the group of Constructivist artists associated with the periodical *Lef*: Varvara Stepanova, Liubov Popova, Aleksandr Rodchenko, Vladimir Tatlin and the Vesnin brothers. Decisively rejecting the old style of dressing, they proposed to substitute it with the new work overall (*prozodezda*), which they defined as 'costume of the present day': by the term work overall they meant various types of professional costume, and in particular sportswear.

The theoretical platform for the Constructivist artists working in the field of costume was provided by Varvara Stepanova, the only one of the group to have specific professional training as a dress-designer. It is through her pronouncements on the pages of the periodical *Lef* and her participation in INKUK, that the theories of Constructivism were transferred into fashion. In 1923 Stepanova decisively affirmed 'It is not a question of general costume, but of costume specifically designed to carry out a particular productive function'[6]. The Constructivist artists followed three basic principles in making the new work overall: functional design, cutting technique and manufacture of the garment. Stepanova's well-tried principles were used in the creation of overalls for surgeons, firemen, pilots and special forms of practical headdress (for example the famous visor created for the sales staff at 'Gosizdat', the state publishing house) in which Stepanova was herself photographed. Not being able to count on mass-production, this group of artists spread their designs through periodicals, design posters, book covers and photomontage. Of primary importance to the Constructivists was sportswear, which had to annihilate and totally substitute everyday clothing, whilst at the same time acquire a style for the workers; these affirmations coincided with the romantic idea, typical of those years, about the significance of gymnastics as a means of attaining a healthy and aesthetic life.

Lamanova and Exter were also concerned with sports attire, including under this heading not only special outfits for players, but also comfortable and light-weight garments like jackets, short coats and the uniform of the pioneers: famous is the jacket designed by Tatlin, which is similar to one of Exter's preceding models – interesting because of the cut and fur trim: the overall by Rodchenko is also well known. The Constructivists retained in the sportswear 'all the decorative themes and trimmings which should have disappeared' in order to allow for a practical suitability of its purpose; moreover it was really in these examples of sportswear that Stepanova and the other stylists included decorative symbols and emblems essential for distinguishing one team from another and the obvious means of recognition for sportswear became colour. A particular sphere of activity in which Popova and Stepanova were involved was fashion shows in which made to measure clothes for women, made with their own, quite simple and comfortable fabrics, as was wanted by European fashion in the Twenties, were shown. In those years Constructivist clothing design could not be reproduced on an industrial scale, but many of their ideas were found realized in the theatre, where they were applied with extraordinary success.

At the beginning of the Thirties, solutions were beginning to be found to the many problems relating to the creation of clothing for the masses: in fact in this period, the construction of new factories, the recuperation of the old centres of production and the foundation of technical institutes for the clothing industry all helped in the radical economic transformation of the country. In the couture sector at the beginning of the Thirties, a personality of major prominence is Nadezda Makarova, a talented pupil of Lamanova. She began her career as a stylist at the Workshop of Contemporary Dress where, abiding by the dictates of her teacher, Makarova sought out beauty in simplicity, and was fascinated by the idea of the interchangeability elements of costume, on a structural basis, that was the creative trend towards the end of the Twenties. Makarova was the first director of the Moscow Fashion House, opened in 1934 in order to create designs suited to mass production. In this new activity this notable designer worked decisively towards the creation of practical and comfortable types of dress suitable for everyday wear and work activity. In individual creations Makarova often emulated popular Russian folk themes, not only in the cut but also in the decorative elements, proportions and style. In 1930 she presented at the international Fur Trade Exhibition in Leipzig, some winter coat designs, jackets and winter hats finished-off with fur and decorated with stripes inspired by the traditional costume of Nency.

Among the stylists of the Thirties was a new figure, Natalya Kiseleva, who, like Popova and Stepanova, revealed a great talent in the creation of sportswear. Kiseleva also created clothes for women in which a geometrizisation of forms was used, bringing them in line with the passion for asymmetric lines, the use of different materials in one dress and the complex finishing characteristic of European fashion. It was not by chance that Kiseleva particularly loved sportswear, she was

The actress A. Khochlova wearing a dress designed by N. Lamanova, 1923.

herself an expert fencer and swimmer. Like the Constructivists who she knew well, Kiseleva kept her sportswear essentially simple and practical, while believing that beauty and elegance were necessary attributes of the athlete's costume.

Among her sketches we find leisure clothes and costumes for fencers and swimmers, some of which are striking in their modernity and similarity to the sports fashions worn nowadays. Some of these are illustrated here: they are witness to the achievements, to date underrated, of an extraordinary group of artists of the post-revolutionary period who exercised an enormous influence on the artistic life of their own and future eras.

1. D. Aranovic, *'Pervaja sitcenabivnaja fabrika v Moskve'* (The first factory of printed cotton in Moscow), in *Iskusstvo odevat'sja* (The art of dressing), 1928, n.1, p.11.
2. Records of the first General Russian Conference on artistic industry, recorded in August 1919, Moscow, 1920, pp.37-38.
3. T. Strizenova, *Iz istorii sovetskogo kostjuma* (From the history of Soviet costume), Moscow, Sovetskij chudoznik, 1978, p.38. T. Strizenova, *Fashion and Revolution*, Milan, Electa, 1979, p.20.
4. Ibidem, pp.50-54.
5. A. Exter, *'V konstruktivnoj odezde'* (In the structure of dress) in *Atel'e*, 1923, n.1, pp.4-5.
6. T. Strizenova, *Iz istorii sovetskogo kostjuma* (From the history of Soviet costume), p.84.

MANUFACTURING DREAMS: TEXTILE DESIGN IN REVOLUTIONARY RUSSIA

John E. Bowlt

The activity of the artist-engineer will become a bridge from production to consumption. Consequently, the artist's organic involvement in industrial production as 'engineer' is proving to be . . . . an essential condition for the *economic* system of Socialism.[1]

In this statement of 1923, the Soviet critic Boris Arvatov, a fervent supporter of Constructivism, epitomized a principal cultural direction of his time – from studio art to industrial design. This was a move favoured by many prominent artists and critics such as Alexander Exter, Alexei Gan, Litbov Popova, Alexander Rodchenko, Varvara Stepanova and Vladimir Tatlin, to mention but a few. However, Arvatov and his colleagues were developing a concept that had been operative as early as 1917, even before, and, to a considerable degree, their actions can be regarded as the culmination to a process. In August, 1918, for example, the Visual Arts Section of the People's Commissariat for Enlightenment (IZO Narkompros) opened a special Sub-Section of Industrial Art under Olga Rozanova to deal precisely with the relationship between 'pure' and 'applied' art. In August, 1919, at the First All-Russian Conference on Industrial Art, the Commisar for Popular Enlightenment, Anatolii Lunacharsky, declared: 'If we are to advance towards Socialism, then we must attach more importance to industry and less to pure art'.[2] At the beginning of 1921 the critic David Arkin expressed this in a different way, affirming that after non-objective painting, the next step was "the *creation of objects*, a constructive, productional art'.[3] Not all avant-garde artists shared this idea and the Suprematist painter Ivan Puni (Jean Pougny), for example, was convinced that the very notion of utilitarian art marked a return to primitive culture.[4] Still by and large, the Revolution encouraged artists and administrators alike to focus attention on industrial design, and, as Nikolai Tarabukin declared, the time was now ripe

not for an art that reproduces the external world,
and touches it up with decorative window-dressing,
but for an art that constructs, that processes our external way of life.[5]

True, for the most part, the Soviet Constructivists remained 'artists' and their sporadic attempts to design buildings, furniture, porcelain, etc., were often as aesthetic and as fanciful as their studio work. This does not detract from the importance of their creative endeavour, and, for example, El Lissitzky's interior designs or Rodchenko's lamps and furniture deserve serious critical attention. However, with the exception of Stepanova, none of the Constructivists in Moscow/Leningrad received any professional training in industrial design, and few of them managed to adjust their focus from two dimensions to three. Despite their desire to 'reconstruct not only objects, but also the whole domestic way of life . . . . both its static and kinetic forms',[6] the full transference of 'art' into 'industrial production' remained a utopian vision. When Tatlin, for example, tried to acquaint engineers with the properties of materials, they completely misunderstood him and suggested he go and teach people how to 'draw nicely'.[7]

Nevertheless, in retrospect, we can distinguish at least one area of industrial activity in which certain artists and designers – Exter, Nadezhda Lamanova, Popova, Rodchenko and Stepanova – did make an exciting contribution after the Revolution, one that affected a broad section of the new society, i.e. textile and clothes design.[8] In fact, these artists created what might be called an "avant-garde of fashion" in the early 1920s and gave much thought to the whole issue of the proletarian style to the paradoxical marriage of *haute couture* and mass taste. While the call for a distinctive, Soviet style of textiles and clothing might seem incompatible with the sorry state of the early Soviet garment industry, we should remember that, from the early 1900s onwards, prominent Russian artists had given attention to the design of clothes and fabrics. To a certain extent, therefore, Popova, Stepanova and the generation that followed them – Olga Bogoslovskaia, Sergei Burylin, Mariia Nazarevskaia, etc. were drawing on an established tradition. The Russian applied arts, including embroidery, weaving and dress making, had been especially vigorous in the 1880s onwards when many professional artists had become interested in peasant artifacts and had attempted to reproduce them according to their own stylistic interpretations. There was nothing very innovative

In the previous and following pages, views of the 'Trechgornaja' manufacturing factory.

about the patterns and forms produced there, although many were charming mixtures of the national style and Art Nouveau, especially at the estates of Abramtsevo (managed by Savva Mamontov), Talashkino (managed by Princess Mariia Tenisheva) and Solomenko (managed by Mariia F. Yakunchikova).[9] Still, they directed attention to the Russian cultural heritage and anticipated the brilliant designs of those artists associated with the St. Petersburg World of Art group and Sergei Diaghilev's Ballets Russes. It is often forgotten that the key painters of Russia's *fin de siecle*, many of them associated with the Ballets Russes, such as Lev Bakst, Alexandre Benois, Ivan Bilibin, Alexander Golovin, Boris Kustodiev and Konstantin Somov, not only painted pictures and illustrated books, but also designed clothes.

Bakst is a case in point, for he contributed much to the development of high fashion and influenced leading designers in the West, including Paul Poiret and Erté. Of course, an immediate source of inspiration for his fashions designs was his own costume resolutions for ballets productions such as *Schéhérazade* and *L'Olseau du feu*, in which he emphasized and exaggerated the body's mobility. Bakst treated the body as the primary organizational element on stage (or in the salon) and hence as the determinant of the costume's expression. This induced him not only to expose the body at strategic points, but also to extend its physical movements outwards and not to conceal them as the 19th century theatrical and social dress had tended to do.

Of course, in his individual dress commissions of c. 1910, Bakst was forced to curtail his exuberance in order to conform to a client's taste, but even in his plainest pieces the absence of the corset and sometimes of the brassiere, the emphasis on the long loose dress with cadential folds and a half-moon base maintained his conception of the female anatomy as a kinetic generator and not as a static figure 8. Unexpectedly, Bakst pointed to important concepts of dress design that the Constructivist designers such as Popova and Stepanova developed later. There is, for example, an uncanny visual resemblance between the sports clothes that Bakst designed for *leux* in 1913 (the action of which was supposed to be taking place in 1925) and Stepanova's *sportodezhda* (sports uniform) of 1923, both relying on functional, undecorated

components and restrained, but, distinctive colouring. Of course, Bakst's *leux* pieces are exceptional, for, by and large, Bakst's costume and dress designs are highly decorative, even histrionic, and we can understand why, in the early years of the Soviet regime people had 'fallen out of love with Bakst and fallen in love with industrial clothing'.[10]

The rapid development from an ornamental to an architectonic conception of fabric and dress design was stimulated by the activities of many avant-garde artists involved directly or indirectly in applied art just before the Revolution. In 1912-13, for example, Natalia Goncharova made patterns for embroideries and over forty designs for ladies' dresses, some of which incorporated abstract motifs. In 1915-16, Olga Rozanova, one of the most original adepts of the abstract system of Suprematism applied her dynamic combinations of colour-planes to textile design. In 1916 the painter Kseniia Boguslavskaia, wife of Puni, co-organizers of the legendary exhibitions 'Streetcar V' (Petrograd, 1915) and '0.10' (Petrograd, 1916-16), exhibited an entire range of designs for embroideries, cushions and handbags to two exhibitions of the Association of Independents (Petrograd) and the World of Art (Petrograd). The culmination to this pre-Revolutionary involvement of the avant-garde in the design of textiles, clothes and related accoutrements, was the series of three specialist exhibitions in Moscow, i.e. 'The Exhibition of Contemporary Decorative Art' (1915). 'The Exhibition of Industrial Art' (1915-17) (both at the Lemercier Gallery) and the 'Second Exhibition of Contemporary Decorative Art' (1917) (at the Mikhailova Salon).

Among the contributions by Exter, Malevich, Popova, Evgeniia Pribylskaia, Puni, Rozanova, Nadezhda Udaltsova, Georgii Yakulov et al., were designs for drapes, cushions, carpets, dresses, handbags and belts – 'a harmonious combination of fabric, colour and design'.[11] Of course, these items were oriented towards a bourgeois, affluent and leisured class, and, while sometimes inspired by peasant motifs (as in the case of Rozanova's dresses), they were certainly not intended for the mass market. Still, it is important to remember that artists such as Exter and Popova, who contributed so much to the fashion consciousness of the new Soviet woman in the early 1920s, drew upon

  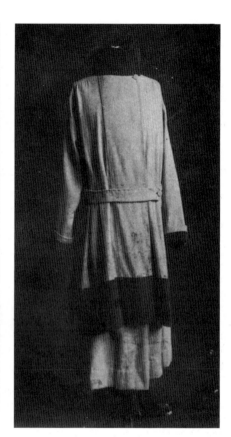

N. Lamanova,
original models
photographed in her
studio, 1923-24.

a rich decorative experience from before the Revolution.

The disruption of the textile industry in the wake of the October Revolution, an industry which, in any case, had been a comparatively backward one despite the large networks of Singer, Rosezweig and Zindel, the traditional reliance of the clothing industry on the individual tailor and seamstress and the sudden disappearance of that very class that had placed private orders – such circumstances meant that clothes design in the new Russia was scarcely contemplated until the conjunction of more clement conditions. Even with the urgent need to create a Red Army uniform, production of a standardized pattern was not really established until after the end of the Civil War in 1921-22. But by 1922-23 the situation was more promising; the inauguration of the New Economic Policy (NEP) in 1921, allowing for a partial return to the free enterprise system, brought forth a new middle-class clientèle; the textile industry began to recover from its stagnation as materials and manpower increased at the main centres of the Trekhgornaia Manufactory, the First State Textile Print Factory and the network in Ivanovo-Voznesensk (the Russian Manchester).

Not least, there was the extraordinary popularity of the tango and the fox-trot, forms of recreation that demanded a new dress – short, loose, free. 'You can't dance the can-can in the costumes of Velasquez', wrote the poet Mikhail Kuzmin in 1923.[12]

Above all, the Constructivists' idea that easel art was a superfluous deception capable only of stylizing reality and not of transforming it quickly gained ground. As the critic Osip Brik asserted in his article 'From Pictures to Textile Prints':

> The studio painting is not only unnecessary to our contemporary artistic culture, but it is also one of the most powerful brakes on its *development* . . . . Only those artists who, once and for all, have recognized productional work in practice not only as an equal form of artistic labour, but also as the only one possible – only these artists can grapple . . . with the solution to the problem of contemporary artistic culture.[13]

As a result, some artists began to describe their abstract compositions no longer as self-sufficient entities, but as models or projects for the creation of new objects. Popova made this quite clear in her statement in the catalogue for the exhibition '5×5 = 25' in Moscow in 1921; 'All the pieces presented here are depictory and should be regarded merely as preparatory experiments towards concrete constructions'.[14] In fact, Popova's textile designs, with their calculated, geometric, repeat patterns, rely considerably on the principles of her abstract painting of 1916 onwards.

At the end of 1922, Popova and Stepanova entered the design section of the First State Textile Print Factory, a combine that had belonged to the German industrialist Emile Zindel. With the exception of Liudmila Maiakovskaia (sister of the poet Vladimir Maiakovsky), who had been working as a designer at the Trekhgornaia Manufactory since 1910, Popova and Stepanova were among the very first women artists to be employed as professional designers in the Russian textile industry. Of course, there had been professional dress designers in St. Petersburg and Moscow before the Revolution who had catered to a restricted circle of customers, orienting their taste towards Paris. One or two of them even managed to adapt their sights to the question of democratic dress – as, for example Lamanova did. A celebrated couturier in Moscow before the Revolution (and a buyer, incidentally, of Goncharova's embroidery and dress designs), Lamanova was one of the few Soviet dress designers to have had experience in this discipline, and, in spite of the abrupt shift from the private commission to the mass ready-to-wear, she produced much important theoretical and practical work on the new dress design. Although she was not as radical as Popova and Stepanova, she understood the needs of the time, as she demonstrated at the First All-Russian Conference on Industrial Art in 1919:

> [Art] must penetrate all spheres of everyday life, it must develop the artistic taste and feeling of the masses. Clothes are one of the most appropriate vehicles for this . . . in the clothing business artists must take the initiative and work to produce very simple but pleasing forms of clothing from simple materials, clothing which will be suitable to the new structure of our working life.[15]

It was a peculiar world that greeted Popova and Stepanova at the First State Textile Print Factory.

Despite the measures taken by IZO Narkompros in 1919-20 to raise the technical competence of textile designers, despite the resonant call among the avant-garde for a constructive and industrial art form, the prevailing kind of design was a pastiche of styles differing little from pre-Revolutionary stereotypes. In some cases this was a florid ornament which bore a remote resemblance to traditional peasant motifs; in other cases, it was a vulgarized Art Nouveau, at best, the design was a simple check.

The ignorance and conservatism that Popova and Stepanova encountered on the factory floor contrasted sharply with the sophisticated declarations of their intellectual colleagues. Some enthusiasts, for example, championed throw-away clothing, referring to the paper underwear which, they alleged, America was already producing.[16] Others advocated nudity as the real equivalent of democracy, an exhortation that accompanied Evenings of the Denuded Body in Moscow in 1922.[17] Actually, the concept of nudity as the most expressive form of 'dress' derived from a theatrical principle that had been much discussed in 1910 – especially by the playwright and producer Nikolai Evreinov who incidentally, became a member of the Atelier of Fashions in Moscow in 1923.[18] Nudity and the case for a totally new look also touched on the wider issue of the 'new body' in the 1910s-20s, i.e. of the need to redesign both the psychology and the physiology of man within the framework of the new economic, political and social structure – a form of biological engineering and artistic prophylaxis that was envisioned by Lissitzky, Malevich, Mikhail Matiushin and many other artists of the time.[19]

Popova brought to the world of textile design a rich and varied artistic training.

By the end of 1922 she had worked as a studio painter, as a poster designer and as a stage designer. She had moved rapidly from Cubism (she studied with Le Fauconnier and Metzinger in Paris in 1912-13) to her 'painterly architectonics' of 1916, she had taken part in major avant-garde exhibitions, and had assumed artistic responsibility for Vsevolod Meierkhold's famous production of *The Magnanimous Cuckold* in April, 1922.

Popova was one of the most austere and principled members of the Russian avant-garde, and, however diverse her activities, she remained faithful to certain basic concepts of form and space. Even though she had limited exposure to applied art, she recognized immediately the distinctiveness of the task before her and, accordingly, she adjusted her conception of 'artistic' space; instead of dealing with a flat, two-dimensional surface (the canvas), she was now concerned with an undulating, three-dimensional solid (the human body); instead of a static quantity which had to be viewed frontally, she was now working on a mobile sculpture to be seen from many angles; instead of a decoration which followed a single, logical impetus, she now needed a design which would still give visual and psychological satisfaction when creased, rucked or mingled with other forms.

To this end, Popova took simple forms, combining them in grids of regular or irregular lines: an enthusiast of jazz (and ballroom dancing), Popova evoked the sense of syncopation and arhythmicality through counterpoints of eccentric compositions – in some cases there are curious anticipations of Op-Art.

That movement was the basis of Popova's art is clear not only from her choice of specific geometric forms (the triangle, the lozenge, the circle) which she assembles in such a way as to produce the sensation of ascension and levitation, but also from her recourse to the psychological 'game'. For example, in one composition of five circles Popova acts as a juggler, interchanging sizes, sequences and combinations. In another, she uses the circle in conjunction with the properties of weight and motif gravitation so that the true sequence of the large circles is disturbed by a vacillation either towards the variable green circle or towards the orange or red. Applied to a piece of clothing, i.e., placed in a condition of movement, these designs lose none of their effectiveness, and even though the wearer may be sitting, the designs continue to 'move'.

There is a clear connection here between Popova's dynamic dresses and the doctrine of Taylorism, industrial gymnastics, and industrial gesticulation being researched concurrently at the Institute of Rhythm in Moscow.

Reprocessing the eurhythmic ideas of Jaques-Dalcroze, the Soviet rhythmists, led by Ippolit Sokolov, affirmed that:

СПОРТИВНЫЙ КОСТЮМ

N. Lamanova,
design sketch for
sportswear, 1925.

The new physical culture is the departure-point for the new productional art. *The artistic design of the labor processes (labor physical culture) is a production art* . . .

Labor gymnastics are a *psycho-physiological gymnastics*.[20]

Clearly, Popova and her Constructivist colleagues were tailoring their costumes to this demand for physical efficiency, agreeing, no doubt, that:

Well-balanced, rhythmical lines exert an influence on the masses, make them more rational, more organized, and stengthen their aspiration towards self-discipline.[21]

Their streamlined designs, theoretically, at least, would have functioned well in the workplace. The problem was that this economy of gesture presupposed a willingness on the part of the masses to understand these principles, i.e. an *active* psychological involvement. But simple, working people, confronted with 'light, air, hygiene, convenience, cleanliness, economy'[22] still wondered where the art was. Even more sophisticated observers such as the design theoretician Alexander Toporkov argued that:

Calculation is possible only on the basis of vital intuition, and one can construct only when one possesses great creative fantasy. A machine . . . is not only intelligent, but also imaginative.[23]

Like Popova, Stepanova was also able to work soberly and pragmatically. Regarding emotion, illusion and ornament as alien to production art, she aspired to eradicate the

ingrown view of the ideal artistic drawing as the imitation and copying of nature; to grapple with organic design and orient it towards the geometrization of forms; to propogate the productional tasks of Constructivism.[24]

In keeping with their wish that the decorative and decorating aspects of clothing be abolished, Stepanova and Popova worked on various types of stereotype clothing – the so called *prozodezhda* (industrial clothing), *spetsodezhda* (special clothing) and *sportodezhda* (sports clothing). Stepanova maintained that each profession – factory worker, doctor, actor, sportsman, etc., – demanded its own costume, which should be constructed according to the norms of convenience and expediency dictated by that profession. The most exciting instance of Stepanova's experiments in this area were her designs for sports clothes incorporating lightness of form (for mobility), economy of material (to restrain the body's temperature) and bright emphatic colours (for identification on the field). They were not mass produced, although Stepanova's design work for Meierkhold's production of *The Death of Tarelkin* in 1922 provided her with the opportunity at least to 'mobilize' her uniforms in a three-dimensional, living environment. Stepanova's husband, Rodchenko, was also active as a textile and clothes designer in the early 1920s and produced his own *prozodezhda* in the form of a worker's coverall; and Tatlin designed a coat and cheap, cut-out suit for everyday wear.

The principle of maximum effect through minimum means, shared by Popova and Stepanova, was counteracted to some extent by the methods of the rival group of textile clothes designers in Moscow attached to the so-called Atelier of Fashions. This establishment catered mainly to the new Soviet bourgeoisie – the *NEPmeny* – of the early 1920s, and although its most serious members, Exter and Vera Mukhina, approached the problem of design with care and imagination, they did not repeat the simplicity and feasibility of Popova and Stepanova.

On the one hand, Exter declared that the dress should consist of simple geometric shapes and that certain materials were appropriate to certain forms; on the other hand, she included fur on sleeves, resorted to Egyptian motifs and incorporated pearl necklaces and fans as ornaments and not as extensions of the body's form and movement. Exter's tendency towards the extravagant attained more striking results in the theatre and cinema, as, for example, in the space movie *Aelita* (1924). True, Exter did design a few clothes for mass consumption, but even here she imbued them with 'arbitrary' elements. The Suprematist circles on her hats and dresses, for example, bring to mind immediately the 'capricious' porthole windows on Grigorii Barkhin's building for the *Izvestiia* Newspaper offices in Moscow in 1927.

However much we praise the projects of Exter, Popova, Rochenko, Stepanova, Tatlin, etc., we

should remember that these were avant-garde experiments and that, lacking the necessary support system of modern industrial and production methods, they were not able to 'liberate technological development from the power of the cliche'.[25] These experiments were part of the total vision of cultural transformation that artists, designers, theatre producers and architects entertained in the 1920s, convinced that their Constructivist ideas were 'democratic', even though, in practical terms, they were at variance with the simple requirements of the mass clientele. There is a certain logic in the fact that all these artists worked simultaneously for the avant-garde theatre and cinema, where the stage or screen acted as a laboratory – confined, concentrated, controlled – for research into the creation of prototypes for the land of the future. The critic and sculptor, Boris Ternovets, wrote in his catalogue essay for the Soviet pavilion at the 'Exposition des Arts Décoratifs' in Paris in 1925:

> Mais la nouvelle culture s'affirme peut-être plus combative, plus intrépide, plus impitoyable à l'égard des formes périmées que partout ailleurs, dans notre Section théâtrale. Loi le problème n'est pas seulement posé; il reçoit sa solution.[26]

Even so the 'solution' was meaningful only in the theatre. Once taken out into everyday life, this 'modern culture' perished – as the critic Boris Brodsky has observed in the context of Rodchenko's furniture designs for Meirkhold's production of *The Bed-Bug* in 1929: 'The sofa-bed was displayed not in a store, but on the stage, as a gibe at everyday life'.[27] It is in this context that the 'Post-Modernism' of the late 1920s-30s, including the figurative textile designs, makes particular sense. Rejecting or, at least, questioning the lessons of their elders, younger designers such as Bogoslovskaia, Burylin and Mariia Nazarevskaia either reverted to a traditional floridity or they treated the textile as a pictorial surface which could transmit a narrative or agitational message. Of course, the new, figurative textiles were a direct response to public demand, although, as the critic David Arkin, made clear, the images were often incongruous, even absurd:

> Unfortunately, this Soviet ornament is, as a rule, characterized by two features; the same

absolute refusal to take into account the subsequent fate of a given fabric (intricate designs on the theme of the Civil War on *kerchiefs* which fold into four) and the poor inventiveness, the primitive monotony in the treatment of the same old simple emblems and allegories . . . . This agitational and didactic subject-matter (tractors and threshing-machines, etc. . .) is, for some reason or another, presented in a stylistic processing of the most archaic kind; contemporary American tractors with internal combustion engines or electric gears are shown on a fabric in a luxurious frame of clusters of grapes straight out of some panneau or furniture fabric from the 18th century.[28]

How do we explain the sudden flowering of the thematic textile in the late 1920s The weight of the traditional claim that the image be narrative is, of course important, but there are also other forces at work. The validity of the Constructivist assumption – that Constructivism was a truly proletarian style – was and is questionable. It became a point of especially heated debate in the wake of the 'Exposition des Arts Décoratifs' in 1925, where it was noticed that textile designers from bourgeois countries (e.g. Sonia Delaunay) were producing patterns for their rich clientèles very similar to those of the Soviet Constructivists. Furthermore, the apologists of the industrial aesthetic such as Arkin, Toporkov and Alfred Kurella came to be regarded not only as blind supporters of Capitalist industry, but also as traitors to the basic concept of art as the bearer of a superimposed, ideological message. A piece of upholstery fabric, it was argued, may carry a motif that has nothing to with the function of the divan, but it may still have a lot to do with class consciousness. One conclusion, therefore, was that 'what they call art (social expediency, etc.) is not art from the Marxist viewpoint'.[29] The transference of traditional symbols of power to proletarian reality was also an important part of the orientation away from Constructivist sparsity to Socialist Realist luxury. It was felt increasingly in the 1930s that the new society had the right to enjoy the privileges that its imperial predecessor had possessed and to manifest the same symbols (e.g. Doric columns on buildings) readily

V. Muchino, elegant outfit, late Twenties, Lamanova Archives, collection Tatyana Strizenova.

Facing and following pages: V. Stepanova, design sketches for costumes for 'The Death of Tarelkin' 1922.

identifiable with power. After all, this was now the dictatorship of the proletariat.

The reaction against Constructivism in the mid-1920s onwards coincided with the reinforcement and consolidation of Soviet industry, especially as the Soviet Union entered the First Five Year Plan in 1929. This meant that some of the problems of organization and production, experienced by the earlier designers, were resolved as more factories began to produce more goods for more people. That is why there are many more examples of 'agit' or thematic textiles than 'abstract' or Constructivist ones – which is not to say that the lessons of the early 1920s were completely lost. Maiakovskaia, for example, continued to create her extraordinarily modern aerographic patterns which today would look quite appropriate in an Italian department store. Natalia Kiseleva, wife of the interior designer Abram Damsky, also produced abstract designs during the 1930s.

However, the trend after 1924-25 was certainly towards the narrative motif – and electrical gadgets (Bogoslovskaia), radio (Lila Raitser), the Red Army and Navy (Vera Lotonina), tourists (Nazarevskaia), pioneers (Oskar Griun) were schematicized and applied to a wide range of objects. As the exhibition demonstrates, this vocabulary was extremely rich, whether practised at the main centres (e.g. the Trekhgornaia Manufactory) or at peripheral factories (e.g. in Kalinin and Serpukhov); and although part of it was clearly ideological (e.g Daria Preobrazhenskaia's *International Communist Youth*), it was not alway successful in communicating the necessary message. The critic Alexei Fedorov-Davydov emphasized this lack of 'socio-political trenchancy'[30] in his long article on textiles in 1931. Actually, many of these textiles designs were used for upholstery, table linens and bathroom accessories rather than for dresses and suits. In fact, photographs of crowd scenes of the 1930s rarely show us a Soviet lady in anything more exciting than a flowered frock, a check blouse or a monochrome overcoat. On the other hand, peasant motifs were sometimes reintroduced and applied to summer blouses and skirts, a rural reference that connected immediately with the larger theme of the countryside in flux as collectivization took place. Still, the problem with this celebration of agricultural, industrial and military achievement was that, as independent compositions, these designs might have appealed, but, as examples of applied textiles, they surely failed; it is hard to imagine, for example, how the larger images such as Raitser's Red Army designs of the early 1930s could have retained the intactness of their message if the material had to be cut, seamed, and creased. In this respect, the miniature motifs such as Bogoslovskaia's *Little Hammers* or Oskar Griun's *Spools* fared much better.

Perhaps, ultimately, the applicability of all these textile designs is now secondary. When all is said and done, we approach these textile designs, both abstract and emblematic, as sources of aesthetic enjoyment, and whether or not they were able to function as dresses, skirts, nightgowns or coats now seems almost irrelevant. Indeed, the Constructivists wish that the artist become an engineer was not entirely fulfilled, but the diversity and imaginativeness of these textile designs indicates, surely, that, in the 1920s and 1930s, the artist began to play a major, innovative role in the visual and semiotic definition of everyday Soviet life.

1. B. Arvatov, *Iskussivo i proizyodstvo*, Moscow; Proletkult, 1926, p. 119.
2. (A. Lunacharsky), 'Rech Narodnogo Komissara prosveshchenia, A. V. Lunacharskogo' in *Pervaia Vserossiiskaia konferentsiia po khudozhestvennoi promyshiennosti avgust 1919*, Moscow: NKP, 1920, p. 63.
3. D. Arkin, 'Izobrazitelnoe iskusstvo l materialnaia kultura' in D. Shterenberg *et. al.*: *Iskusstvo y proizvodstve*, Moscow NKP, 1921, No. 1, p. 18.
4. J. Puni, 'Iskusstvo zhizni' in *Spolokhi*, Berlin, 1921, No. 1, pp. 37-38.
5. N. Tarabukin, *Ot molberta k mashine*, Moscow: Rabotnik prosveshchenila, 1923, p. 44.
6. Ibid., pp. 23-24.
7. I. M. (-Ivan Matsa), 'Khudozhniki i proizvodstvo' in *Vestnik iskussty*, Moscow, 1922, No. 5, p. 25.
8. Among recent sources of information on the position of the textile and garment industry in early Soviet Russia the following titles should be mentioned: T. Strizhenova: *Iz istoril sovetskogo kostriuma*, Moscow: Sovetskii khudozhnik, 1972 (translated into Italian as *Moda e rivoluzione* Milano: Electa, 1979); I. Yasinskaia: *Sovetskie tkani 1920-1930-kh godov*, Leningrad: Khudozhnik RSFSR, 1977 (American version: *Revolutionary Textile Design*, New York: Studio, 1983); *Art into Production*, Catalogue of exhibition of Soviet textiles, fashion and ceramics 1917-1935 at the Museum of Modern Art, Oxford, England, 1984; R. Messina: 'Spaziarono su orizzonti infiniti' in *Realià sovietica*, Roma, 1986, maggio-giugno, pp. 68-76; *Journal of Deporative and Propaganda Arts*, Miami, USA, 1987, No. 5 special issue on Russian and Soviet design with articles by

БРАНДАХЛЫСТОВА

N. Adaskina, W. Salmond, T. Strizhenova, et al., on textiles and fashion). For commentary on the comparative context of Russian and Soviet textile design see the two volumes by G. and R. Fanelli: *Il tessuto Art Nouveau* and *Il tessuto Art Deco e anni trenta*, Florence: Cantini, 1986.

9. On Abramtsevo see D. Kogan, *Mamontovskii kruzhok*, Moscow: Izobrazitelnoe iskusstvo, 1970; N. Beloglazova; *Abramtsevo*, Moscow: Sovetskaia Rossila, 1981; for a generic discussion of the activities at Abramtsevo see D. Gavrilovich: 'Un caleidoscopio sonoro ovvero la sintesi delle arti in Russia' in *Ricerche di Storia dell'Arte*, Roma, 1985, No. 25, pp. 17-28. On Talashkino see J. Bowlt: 'Two Russian Maecenases, Savva Mamontov and Princess Tenisheva' in *Apollo*, London, 1973, December, pp. 444-53; for the kind of peasant motifs that were incorporated into the textiles produced at Abramtsevo and Talashkino see the album *Broderies der paysannes de Smolensk exécutées sous la direction de la Princesse Marie Ténichév*, Paris: Librarie centrale des beaux arts, and Chicago: G. Broes van Dort, no date, On Solomenko see W. Salmond: 'The Solomenko Embroidery Workshops' in *Journal of Decorative and Propaganda Arts*, op. cit.

10. V. Mass, 'Pankrasy novogo fronta' in *Zrelishcha*, Moscow, 1922, No. 10, p. 9. Quoted in E. Rakitina (compiler): *Khudozhnik, stsena, ekran*, Moscow: Sovetskii khodozhnik, 1975, p. 158.

11. M. Liakhovskaia, 'Vystavka sovremennogo dekorativnogo iskusstva' in *Mir zhenshchiny*, Moscow, 1915, No. 15-15, p. 30.

12. M. Kuzmin (1923). Quoted in V. Berendeev: 'Tush v chest direktrisy" in *Yunost*, Moscow, 1975, No. 9, p. 107.

13. O. Brik, 'Ot kartiny k sittsu' in *Lef* Moscow, 1924, No. 2, pp. 30-31.

14. L. Popova, untitled contribution to the catalogue of the exhibition '5×5 = 25', Moscow, 1921, unpaginated.

15. N. Lamonova, 'O masterskikh sovremennykh khudozhestvennykh kostiumov' in *Pervaia Vserossiiskaia*, op. cit., pp. 37-38.

16. Yu Annenkov, 'Estestvennoe otpravlenie' in E. Kuznetsov (ed.): *Arena*, Petersburg, Krug, 1924, p. 114.

17. E. Kan, 'Telo l odezhda' in *Zrelishcha*, 1922, No. 7, p. 16.

18. See, for example, the collection of articles edited by N. Evreinov, *Nagota na stsene*, St. Petersburg; Butkovskaia, 1910. This collection contains the 'Manifesto on Nudity' by the artist I. G. Miasoedov.

19. It is reasonable to assume that the *New Man* that Lissitzky designed and depicted as Figure No. 10 in his set of lithographs for the opera *Victory over the Sun* (i.e. *Die plastische Gestaltung der elektro-mechanischen Schau 'Sieg uber die Sonne'*. Hannover: Leunis und Chapman, 1923) represented his vision of the new, streamlined, automated inhabitant of the perfect Socialist state. The robotic figures that Malevich painted in his landscapes of the late 1920s and early 1930s seem also to represent the new human being, physically and psychologically changed. Matlushin's experiments on the widening of our visual perception to 360 derives from this fundamental wish to redesign humanity.

On the question of art and prophylaxis see A. Ivanov: *Iskusstvo Opyt sotslalno-refleksologicheskogo analiza* Moscow: Proletkult, 1927, especially pp. 98-101.

20. I. Sokolov: *Sistema trudovol gimnastiki*, Moscow, 1922 (publishing-house not indicated), p. 5.

21. K. Zalevsky, *Iskusstvo i proletariat*, Moscow: Vserossiiskii Tsentrainyi ispolnitelnyi komitet sovetov R. S. K. i Krasnykh deputatov, 1918, p. 47.

22. A. Mikhailov, *Izo iskusstyo rekonstruktiynogo perioda*, Moscow-Leningrad: Ogiz-Izgiz, 1932, p. 205.

23. A. Toporkov, 'Forma tekhnicheskaia i forma khudozhestvennaia' in *Iskusstvo v prolzvodsyve*, op. cit., p. 29. Also see Toporkov's essay under the same title in his book *Tekhnicheskii byt i sovremennoe iskusstvo* Moscow-Leningrad: Gosudarstvennoe izdatelstvo, 1928.

24. V. Stepanova. Quoted in Strizhenova, *Iz istorii sovetskogo kostiuma*, op. cit. p. 97.

25. B. Arvatov: 'Iskusstvo v sisteme proletarskol kultury' in V. Bliumenfeld, et al. (eds.): *Na Putiakh iskusstva*, Moscow: Proletkult, 1926, p. 25.

26. B. T. (-Boris Ternovets): 'En guide d'introduction' in catalog of the 'Exposition des Arts Décoratifs', 1925, i.e. *Exposition de 1925, Section URSS Catalogue*, Paris, 1925, p. 19.

27. B. Brodsky, 'The Psychology of Urban Design in the 1920s and 1930s' in *Journal of Decorative and Propaganda Arts*, op. cit.

28. D. Arkin, 'Iskusstvo veshchi' in I. Novich, et al., *Ezhegodnik literatury i iskusstva na 1929 god*, Moscow; Komakademiia, 1929, p. 455. Also see Arkin's book *Iskusstvo bytvol veshchi*, Moscow: Ogiz-lzogiz, 1932, pp. 151-60.

29. Mikhailov, op. cit., p. 205. Mikhailov is criticizing A. Kurella's book, i.e. *Krasivaia zhizn*, Moscow: Molodaia gvardila, 1929.

30. A Fedorov-Davydov, 'Iskusstvo textilla' in P. Novitsky (ed.): *Izofront, Klassovaia borba na fronte prostrantsvennykh iskusstv, Sbornik statei obedineniia 'Oktiabr'*, Moscow-Leningrad; Ogiz, 1931, pp. 69-101. This quotation is from p. 77. The article has been reprinted in A. Fedorov-Davydovs: *Russhoe i Sovetskoe iskusstvo Satati i ocherki*, 1975, pp. 184-205.

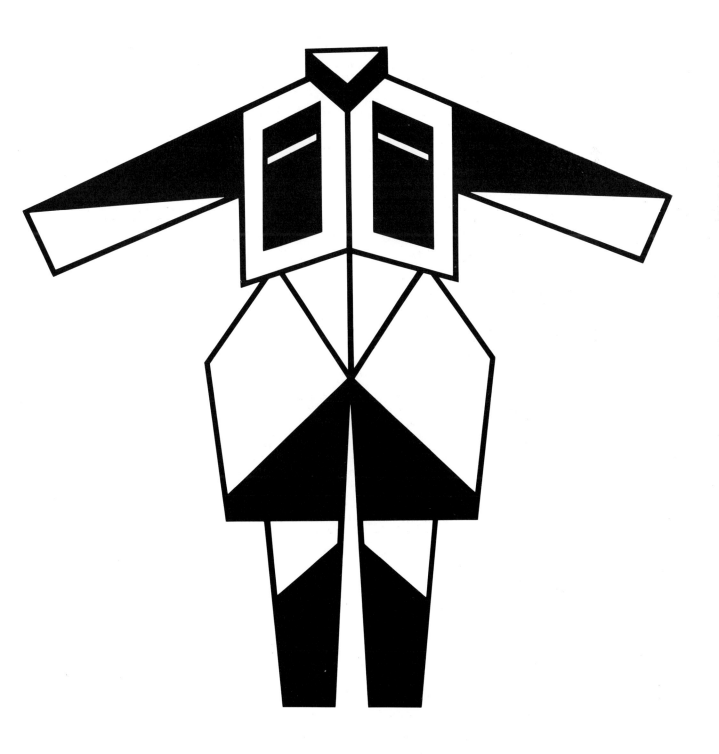

*Moscow at the
beginning of the
eighteenth century:
view of the
'Kamennyu' bridge,
Anonymous
painter, from a
watercolour by
George de la
Barthes, engraving,
Moscow, Literary
Museum.*

WHEN FASHION RETURNED TO COSTUME

Fabio Ciofi degli Atti

Up until the compulsory introduction in 1705 of dress 'after the German' or rather Western dress, the history of Russian clothing follows a curious road: from costume to fashion. From 1920-1930 however, it explores a similar path to that now traced in France and England, of fashion turning back to costume. The semantics that circumscribe the concepts of costume and fashion have been described, with penetrating accuracy, by Levi-Pisetzky. '(. . .) With regard to costume we principally mean the term in its significance as a way of dressing which appeared in our language as early as the sixteenth-century and it should be remembered that, implicit in the expression, was usually a reference to a type of durability as well as a certain uniformity: i.e., popular costume, ecclesiastical costume and court costume (. . .). In contrast the word fashion, introduced in Italy towards the middle of the seventeenth-century, brings to mind a lively image of transience, variability and novelty (. . .)'[1].

The Russian *plat'e* (from the Polish *placie*, cloth), comparable to the Indo-European *costume* (it was first used with an inherent negative connotation, synonymous with ragged and perhaps foreign styled clothing) had replaced the indigenous term when the anonymous writer of the *Domostroj*[2] in the mid-16th century adapted it to signify 'all that we wear, excluding underwear and footwear'[3]. The term fashion first appears – and is in this case symbolic – in the seventeen twenties, during the reign of Tsar Peter I, as a word borrowed not so much directly from French, and certainly not from Latin, but from German. The word *kostyum*, as well as having a Latin origin, was derived from the French *costume*, and is first encountered in the first quarter of the 18th century, meaning both clothes for the stage and the masked ball.

The abandonment of costume – which accompanies the end of feminine reclusion in the *Terem* (a kind of women's quarters situated in the highest, and therefore most hidden, part of the palace) – in order to keep abreast of the capricious changes in fashion, clearly shows that intricacy which, even in Russia, entangles society, politics, economics and culture and which played an unquestionable role in the history of costume.

The 'current usage', of fashion that is, became widespread when first Italian and then other European cities, returned to the old vocation of trading, transforming themselves into commercial centres. This greatly stimulated the output of artisans in agricultural areas whose methods of working had previously been the cause of the sharp divide between city and country production. Thus the urban countryside changed. Vegetable gardens and stables vanished, the road now became the way to the market, small shops and fairs adapted to a new social life, and everywhere one was invited to stop and look at the abundance of goods which spilled out into the cobbled streets and promenades. A role became assigned to fashion and competition developed to display one's social superiority and to flaunt clothes of refined elegance, extravagant with materials and gaudily luxurious.

The Russian urban agglomerations were, for the most part, isolated from commercial streets, not solely because of a lack of prosperity. Another reason why thy did not emerge from the manorial economic state was because they entrusted their birth, growth and decline to the political-military fortunes of the prince, who maintained the urban population as artisans in order to provide exclusively for the needs of his own luxurious life. At the end of the nineteenth century, the capital Moscow was still similar to a large village – as the people of St. Petersburg contemptuously described it – since every house, whether it be an artisan's workshop or a nobleman's residence, was self-sufficient, equipped with vegetable gardens, pasture, and orchards. This was above all noticeable in the topography of the area. Deprived of any juridical state whatsoever, Moscow had a radiocentric configuration, in which the stronghold of the prince was the central pivot of urban design, an unchanging social framework for an eternal citizenry. It was a scheme exemplified on the symbolic model of Jerusalem, almost arising from the temple of Solomon, an emanation of Christian divinity, and an image of a spectacular celestial haven. The houses and isolated cottages were small individual units, without any form of collective life, and were scattered over a vast territory. Houses were surrounded by fences, with windows which faced inwards, making the street the domain of domestic animals, and there was not yet a place for social gatherings, like the communal centres or the walks and squares of the West where the impetus and passion of the people overflowed – symbols of civic rights. If, therefore, fashion is a

*The people of
Novgorod at prayer
(detail from an icon
of 1467), tempera
painting on panel,
Novgorod, Museum
of History and
Architecture.*

typically urban phenomenon, there was no reason at all why it should have existed in the Russian cities, where the invariability of this structural model subtended an inner economic and social staticity, unaltered since the foundation, in 1703, of the new capital St. Petersburg. It seems strange, therefore, when analyzing the terminology adopted by theorists on Soviet dress, in the initial post-revolutionary years and, afterwards, by the Constructivists, that the word 'fashion' is omitted and used – laden with negative significance – solely in reference to the West. Lamanova states: '(. . .) The new, present-day Russian reality does not want to submit to the tyranny of fashion nor to a lack of any standards (. . .)'[4]. Exter proclaims: '(. . .) In fashion which is changeable according to commercial whims, we must oppose intricate and beautiful clothing for the sake of simplicity'[5].

The clothing of the new era was defined with the words *kostyum* and *plat'e*, almost as if to signify the irreversibility and the immutability of social relations now overturned, as if in the memory of these traditions one could justify the revolutionary caesura. Thus the caftan and the *sarafan* reappeared and were considered to be popular, indigenous clothing. However, this was historically untrue (their etymology show the garments go back to a Persian-Turkish origin) but this false history was useful in combating the cultural value of dress in its double role of dominance and magical-ritual practice. It is underprivileged people, without any military, political or cultural importance who tend to imitate the behaviour and even the way of dressing of the dominant community; a kind of susceptible magical prototype, which, if copied, produces and generates an imitation of reality. The young Soviet state not only had to project itself as a beacon of civilization but had to prove that wearing foreign clothes did not represent an act of political, religious or moral subjection. This episode is not unique in Russian history; German dress, restricted up until the end of the 17th century but triumphant with Peter I, was again banned by Paul I (at the end of the 18th century); Alexander I (at the beginning of the 19th century) vetoed the revolutionary *pantalon* of the *sans culottes*; and more recently we have witnessed an intolerance towards fashions vaguely defined as 'Western'.

Battle outside Novgorod, Museum of History and Architecture.

Designs for the New Red Army uniform: pastrano caftan and bogetyrka summer jacket.

It was not by chance therefore that the military uniform of the Red Army was reminiscent of Medieval Russia, with the *bogatyrka*, the famous Budjonnyi hat that Kustodiev, the painter, unfamiliar with its Persian origins, since he was a typical Venetian, probably drew from a Norwegian ikon of the XV century, and the accompanying *pastrano-caftan* was not so much Russian as Turkish-Polish. Likewise a dress by Lamanova, inspired by the taste for folk art and awarded a prize at the Paris Exhibition of Decorative Arts in 1925, only testified to the flame of exoticism in Russia, very soon put out, with the *mujik* jacket, developed by Bakst from 1909 onwards with the costumes for the Diaghilev's Ballet Russe. This was a fashion mocked by Proust in *Sodom and Gomorrah*, the story of a certain princess Yourbeletoff who appeared on the scene in the beautiful world of Paris, patroness of 'all these great men – Bakst, Nijinsky, Benois and Stravinsky – adorned from head to foot with an enormous dangling plume, unknown to the Parisians, who will all immediately try and imitate this, as if in the very belief that these same Russian dancers have carried this marvellous creation in their plentiful luggage as their most precious treasure'[6].

It is even worth remembering that the clothing superimposed by Exter, judged extravagant but which later caught the eye of the Japanese, contrary to other European countries, found distant similarities in Russian history, since the disparity in dressing, marked socially by the length of the tunic, was based not on the style, but on the number of clothes and on the quality of their material that the noble boasted. The English poet and diplomat Giles Fletcher, invited to Moscow in 1588 in order to conclude a commercial treaty and an alliance with the Czar Fedor Joannovic, gives a rare description of the costume of a wealthy lady and a boyar in his *Of the Russian Commonwealth*: as to the lady 'The *opasen* dress is long and usually red, with rich and pretentious sleeves reaching to the ground, fastened at the front by large gold, or at least gilded silver buttons similar to Greek walnuts. Under the collar is sewn another costly fur, wide and big enough to cover half the back. Under the *opasen* or dress is worn another garment, called a *letnik*, with stitching on the front, with big wide sleeves, of which the half that reaches the elbow is usually made up of gold

brocade; still under this they wear a *ferez* loose and buttoned to the feet.' (The *ferez is a long tunic identical for both sexes. The etymology is derived from the Turkish feredze* garment.) As to the boyar himself: 'Under the embroidered shirt (in summer and indoors this is all they wear) he wears the *zipun*, or else a light silk garment reaching to the knee and buttoned down the front; in other words a caftan, or else a straight garment with a Persian type sash in which are kept knives and forks. The caftans are usually of gold brocade and reach to the ankles. Over the caftan they wear a loose garment of expensive silk lined with fur, decorated with gold braid, called a *ferjaz* (. . .) and still under this is a garment of fine material or Chinese silk '[7]. The *zipun* is taken directly from the Venetian *zipon* or jacket, or is indirectly transmitted from the Greek *zipouni*.

The comparison with Exter's explanatory notes on a two-piece walking suit is enlightening: 'Underneath, is a tunic with ample sleeves, made of heavy bright lilac silk. Over this is a long cassock without sleeves in chamois or in gold coloured cloth. Decorations in skins are attached to the wide reversible or lilac sash and to the border of the tunic. A shawl collar.'[8]. In an elegant garment the famous painter superimposed on a princess two overcoats of striped and contrasting colours, with abundant and falling sleeves, an almost sarcastic, sardonic, sneer at their social symbolism: the emphasis on the impossibility of carrying out any manual work. The contrast with the Constructivism of Stepanova and Popova could not have been more obvious. The idea of the uniform, even though egalitarian and functional, replaced the search for individual expressiveness, and had an even greater effect on the history of costume in Russia. In contrast to the sumptuary laws prevalent in other parts of Europe such as Italy, which tended to oppose luxury, uniform in Russia, sometimes distanced from the concept of egalitarianism, but without undue formality, meant that social distinctions in style were very immediate and perceptible, for example in clothing, in Moscow, where the magical-ritual function of costume persisted for a long time. Regulations were laid down and rigidly followed – the arbitrary ukase of Peter the Great is not the only episode – and as such curbed one of the driving forces of fashion, imitation. The nobility, in fact, stimulate and use

N. Lamanova, dress inspired by folk costume and decorated with hand woven material, which won a Grand Prix at the International Exhibition of Decorative Arts in Paris 1925.

*K. Golejzovskij,
Boris Erdman's
costume from
'Foxtrot', 1923.*

ДЕТИ

A. Ekster, over-dress inspired by a Japanese original, Spring 1923.

V. F. Stepanova, design sketches for costumes for 'The Death of Tarelkin' 1922.

novelty in order to distinguish themselves from subordinate classes, but they in turn, not adverse to flaunting their own pecuniary state, imitated it, goading the nobility to hunt for new signs of distinction and a new way of dressing, that perpetuated the disparity.

The social motivations of this unusual post-revolutionary return to costume are multiple. First, as far as we are concerned, must come the devaluation of money, at least up until the adoption of the NPE (New Political Economy 1921-1922): in a society in which the non-circulation of brand names on the market corresponds to the non-circulation of money, the clothes-image is only an indication of the social function of the individual inside the State structure. Also, education defined in 1923 as 'a unity with work' backed up this devaluation of the traditional scale of values, with a worthy aspiration to eliminate the dichotomy between manual and intellectual work, conveying 'the general scientific foundations of all production methods, until the trainee can concretely use the elementary instruments of all trades'[9]. There is then a belief, ingenuously practical, in the new technical products: the subdivision of work, the assembly line and a faith that is manifested in *masinizm* (mechanization), worship of Taylorism and the machine, uninfluenced by machine or man. The manifesto of FEKS (Workshop of Eccentric Actors, 1922), reads: 'Culture = Europe, Technology = America, or Americanization, the funeral parlour'[10], In 1923 Foregger composed the *Dance of the Machines*; in 1919-1920 Tatlin constructed a model of the *Monument to the Third International*; for the *Death of Tarelkin* (1922) by Suchovo-Kobylin, Meyerhold, in the interrogation scenes, constructed from real machines 'humans' to play the policemen who interacted with one another in an exaggerated, mechanistic way. Clothing had to be functional, hygienic and above all mass-reproducible, and so the structure of clothing was made up of simple geometric shapes, easily assembled, clothing that drew beauty not from esoteric decoration but from its suitability to its functions, and 'from the perfection of the machine-stitched seams'[11].

The motivations of the social order are not however sufficient to explain the Constructivist school of thought, since the theoretical-esoteric diathesis can not be considered separately from the work instigated by Stepanova and Popova. If one wished to try out the hypothesis that the approach to Constructivist overalls has to start with the Saussurian dichotomy of language, that of social prescriptives, and words, as an individual act of expression. Popova and Stepanova seemed to reject the single concrete acts of the word, almost as if – together –

they could construct an individual, expressive or poetic system, isomorphic to the concept of fashion. On the contrary, they wanted to emphasize the importance of material as a means of expression realized in linguistic statements and distinguishing the languages' according to specific functions or specific semantic skills which corresponded to different practices: a practical finalization of the *prozodezda*. In tracing the boundary marks between the linguistic and the stylistic, it seems that the two Constructivists totally released the poetry in the linguistic and improved the stylistic, in the social and universal rules of languagL[12].

The same Stepanova wrote in 1921: 'Style as an organized form in an era. . . loses its sense of industrial culture in the century; and in fact, the external form no longer has a stable value, because of its modification and productive necessity. Only the principle and process are relevant for the realization of the aim for which a given manufactured article is destined'[13].

In their manuscript, in which resides not only the function, destination and essence of manufacture, but also the aesthetic-formal principles, Stepanova and Popova do not differ from Vygostkian theories on the function exercised by extra-formal materials on the formalization process and the simultaneous action exercised by form in the production of the artistic object, where for form one must not mean just an external covering, a mouth that engulfs the fruit, but an active principle of re-elaboration and counterbalance of the material itself[14], which the Constuctivists define as 'tectonic'.

N. Foregger, Mechanical Dancer, 1923.

The organization in praesentia (syntax) of the linguistic elements, must have a technological significance, which justifies the structure: by which the value of practical, manufactured clothing is adapted to the activity with which it is involved, and by which the significance of every decoration is not a reference code. In fact it is shown that the specific structuring of the material participates in the production of the sense of the work – in our case identifiable with the finality – by which it is again shown that the formal organization possesses a specific semantic function of its own. Highly suggestive but paradoxical assumptions, since clothing was loosing its essential connotations: in order to be both an expression of individuality and conformism, to no longer be a lucid exhibition in itself, an instrument of communication for the individual, a loving call, or an aesthetic search or affirmation of social superiority, but instead a return to rationalized dressing for the technocrats of a world frozen and aseptic, deprived of pleasure, against which in 1929 the little-bourgeois Majakovskian *Cimex*, Prisypkin, let out an anguished cry of protest.

The paradox of this open utopia unveiled itself completely half way through the Twenties, when monetary reforms accelerated the development of economic mechanisms and the working class found itself isolated on the assembly line. The revolutionary law was abolished in favour of a legality based on normal civil and penal codes, and the bureaucratic pyramid was re-built. Dress was of a new social denotation, with even more virulence, since the refined peasant and young law-maker nourished by an age-old distrust of culture, wanted to surround themselves, and be corrupted by, emblems and power, which identified a way of life from which they had been excluded for centuries. Taking possession of this was easy since, by leaving the structure intact, they could alter their behaviour merely according to it's face value.

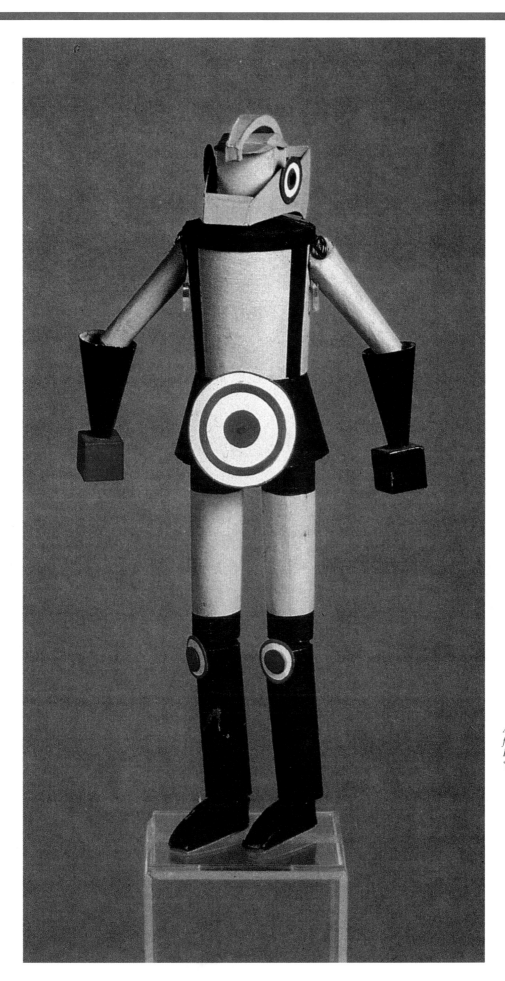

A. Ekster, puppet for Jakov Protazanov's film 'Aelita', 1924.

N. Lamanova, dress inspired by folk costume and decorated with hand woven material, 1923.

1. Rosita Levi Pisetzky, *Costume and fashion in Italian society*, Torino, Einaudi, 1978, p.5

2. Domostroj: a compendium of behaviour, dating back to the VI century, which the good Moscow courtesan had to observe in society and family. The *Domostroj* is the most precious source on customs and costume in the Moscow of the sixteenth century.

3. Vladimir Dal, *Tolkovyj slovarzivogo velikorusskogo jazyka* (Dictionary of the great living language of Russia), 1863-1866, reprinted in Moscow, 1955.

4. Nadezda Lamanova, *Sovremennaja odezda* (Modern Dress), in *Krasnaja niva* (Campo rosso), n.27, 1923.

5. Aleksandra Exter, '*Prostata i prakticnost v odezde*' (Clothing must be simple and practical), in *Krasnaja niva* (Campo rosso), n.21, 1923.

6. Marcel Proust, *Sodome et Gomorrhe*, Pleaide, Paris, 1954, p.743.

7. Gilles Fletcher, *O russkom gosudarstve* (Of the Russian commonwealth), St. Petersburg, 1908, pp.125-127.

8. Quoted by Tatyana Strizenova in *Fashion and Revolution*, Milan, Electa, 1979, p.52.

9. *Formative systems in Europe: Equality and inequality in the Soviet scolastic system*, Fabio Ciofi degli Atti, Milan, Franco Angeli Editor, 1981, p.118.

10. Grigorij Kozincev, Georgij Krizickij, Leonid Trauberg, Sergej Jutkevic, *Ekcentrizm – 1922*. Translated in *Theory of the revolutionary cinema: the Twenties in the USSR*, by Paolo Beretto, Milan, Feltrinelli, 1975, p.226.

11. Varvara Stepanova, *Kostyum segodnjasego dnja-prozodezda* ('Today's Fashion is the work overall'), in *Lef*, n.2, 1923.

12. For relations between linguistic and avant-garde theory in Russia, see Franco Ferrario's *Theory of literature in the USSR 1900-1930*, Rome, Editori Riuniti, 1977. An interesting and little noted thesis, in which we are advised that the writer is Grigorij Vinokur, *Poetika, lingvistika isociologija* (Linguistic and sociological poetry), in *Lef*, n.3, translated into Italian in *Rassegna Sovietica*, n.2, April-June 1965.

13. Varvara Stepanova, *Obscaja teorija konstruktivizma* (The general theory of Constructivism), a catalogue of the exhibition *Rodchenko and Stepanova: on the origins of Constructivism*, Milan, Electa, 1984.

14. L.S.Vygotskij, *Psikhologija iskusstva*, Moscow, 1928. Published in Italian in L.S.Vygotskij's *Psicologia dell'arte* (Psychology of art), introduction by A.N. Leontev, Rome, Editori Riuniti, 1972.

M. Orlova, travelling suit, end of the Twenties.

АТЕЛЬЕ МОД
1923

Inside the Moscow 'Fashion Studio', 12, Petrovka Sreet, 1923.

O.Seniceva, director of the Moscow 'Fashion Studio'.

Dress designed by V. Von Meck at the 'Contemporary Art' Exhibition Saint Petersburg, 1902.

THE SCIENCE OF DRESSING FROM THE INDUSTRIAL WORKSHOP: THE RUSSIAN ACADEMY OF ARTISTIC SCIENCE AND COSTUME – A SUMMARY

Nicoletta Misler

Two Soviet periodicals can be identified as characterizing the polarity of discussion on Soviet fashion in the Twenties and Thirties: the periodical *Atel'e* (Atelier)[1] and *Svejnaja promyslennost (The Clothing Industry)*[2]. Both expressed in different ways the theoretical problem of fashion as a link between clothing, *costume* and daily life, and they both resolved this problem by defining fashion as a link between clothing and art, technology and science.

When the first (and only) edition of the periodical *Atelier* was published in 1923 by the Moscow Union of Clothing Firms, Soviet women, faced with the periodical's very elegant colour reproductions of high fashion designs, after having being so long repressed by the hardships of war communism and civil war, must have felt entitled to such luxurious fantasies of bourgeois elegance.

The first real fashion magazine, after the October Revolution (published purposefully under the New Economic Policy), sanctioned the success gained by the artists Aleksandra Exter[3] and Vera Muchina[4] in collaboration with the stylists Nadezda Lamanova and Evgenija Pribylskaja[5], by including the designs made for the homonymous Atelier of fashion; an original, luxuriously furnished, workshop, in the centre of Moscow, where the designs shown were also presented at the All-Russian Exhibition of Art in Industry[6]. With the definition 'art in industry' (chudozestvennaja promyslenost) the possibility of expanding production of artistically orientated craftsmen was intended.

In fact, while the unique pieces created by the Workshop of Contemporary Dress were presented in the artisan section of the Exhibition, a display of design prototypes by A. Exter for the Moscow clothing industry was staged in the industrial sector. A.Exter, who had played a part in the decoration scheme of the exhibition hall (headquarters of the Russian Academy of Artistic Science) was certainly the most representative figure of the trend and was in fact involved with two theoretical articles, the first, 'In search of new clothing'[7] at the *Exhibition of Art in Industry* and the second, 'In the structure of clothing'[8] in the periodical *Atelier*.

The periodical *Atelier* was anything but a simple women's magazine and famous names contributed to it, like the well-known producer Nikolai Evreinov (from Paris) who lent himself to the feminine game of fashion, in a refined article on the significance of chic, which distinguished a Parisian lady from a lady of Berlin or Petrograd[9]. Evreinov then competently discussed the latest trends of the Paris season with regard to textiles, colours and styles of clothes.

This review confirmed that the subject of fashion was a topic for serious debate in the Soviet Union at that time, so much so that the *troika*, A. Exter, V. Muchina and N. Lamanova (to whom was added E Pribylskaja[10], as an embroidery specialist) were associated not with tailoring or dressmaking workshops, but with artistic workshops like the *Workshop of Contemporary Dress* and the one for *Experimental Textile Colouring*[11]. These two workshops more or less depended institutionally on the prestigious Russian Academy of Artistic Science (RAC*h*N)[12], the same body that had organized the Exhibition of Art in Industry. In this academy, whose programme had been elaborated upon by among others, Anatolij Lunacarskij and Wassily Kandinsky, research was carried out on the potential synthetic relationships between different artistic expressions, trying to verify them experimentally in specific workshops.

Dress design was considered one of those passing things and the two workshops of contemporary dress and textile colouring were constantly experimenting in that sort of work. Evidence of this is found in the words with which the RAC*h*N attributed a testimony of merit to the Atelier of fashion in Moscow at the Exhibition of Art in Industry, for having achieved 'joyful results in colours, the line of the clothes and for the refined interpretation of the rapport between the living person, the material and the artistic form, in the designs exhibited[13].

What clothing had to represent for the theorists of RAC*h*N, was the synthesis between the artistic raw material and its expression in the three-dimensional movement of the human figure, and this stemmed from one of the most important aspects of the research organized by Kandinsky for the psycho-philosophical section of the RAC*h*N. However the synthetic ambitions of the periodical *Atelier* went further. In its editorial, it was affirmed that the aim of the periodical was to 'embrace together daily life (byt), art and industry[14].

Therefore the periodical concentrated not just on clothes, but on all visible aspects of daily life. In an extension of the fashion concept, so topical for us today, it examined: 'the external aspect and

Models from the Moscow clothing industry at the Industrial Art Exhibition.

style of buildings, the decoration of rooms, interior furnishing, furniture, chinaware, glassware, crystal, bronzes, carpets, woven lace, the working of textiles, embroidery'[15].

This acknowledgement constituted, in part, the culmination, or a contemporary version, of the attempts to integrate different aspects of arts and crafts, re-qualifying them artistically (on the designs of Ruskin and Morris), that had been undertaken in the artistic community by Abramcevo and Talaskino before the October Revolution[16], and brought up to date by the Contemporary Art enterprise in St Petersburg (1902)[17], in which individual artists, from Lev Bakst to Alexandre Benois, designed individual settings (from the boudoir to the tea-room) and the Baron Vladimir Von Mech, one

of the movement's financiers, exhibited splendid clothes.

Twenty years later, the same Baron Von Meck appeared as a contributor to the periodical *Atelier* with an article on 'Clothing and the Revolution'[18]. As someone with a profound knowledge of the history of costume, Von Meck examined the changes that took place during the French Revolution and finally expressed his opinion on the debate about the new Soviet clothing, the *prozodezda* (work overall), affirming that if the conception was interesting in theory, it did not seem to have produced great results in practice.

If Van Meck's rejection of the *prozodezda* (work overall) is understandable, one needs to recognize that the designs created in the Atelier of fashion

Model published in 'Atelier', n.1, 1923, dress worn by the opera singer K. Novikova.

and illustrated in the periodical, were a long way from being designs for the masses, but rather they represented unique pieces of high fashion: from those theatricals like Exter and Muchina to those that used refined craft materials like Pribylskaja. The position of the *Atelier* with regard to the work overall was expressed particularly in the writing of Alexandra Exter, and seemed to reproduce the dichotomy between production-artists and followers of Kandinsky, those interested in the function of the artistic object, and others led by their emotions. Exter underlined, in fact, the psychological significance of the work overall and affirmed that numerous rhythms were sought in the form of clothing destined for mass-production[19].

The attention to rhythm (above all in the psychological sense) as a co-ordinating element, brings us back to the research being carried out at the RAChN on Art movement. Under this heading is included both the study of gymnastic rhythm and dance (in the choreography workshop) and the possibility of the scientific visualization of rhythm through graphics, cinema and photography[20]. Rhythm as an autonomous artistic expression in the confines of diverse disciplines like the psychological graphic representation of individual creativity has similarities with the analysis of the effect of clothing on the psyche. This was the thread running though Mikhail Kuzmin's article on theatrical costume in *Atelier*[21] in which the hypothesis was put forward that clothing can alter gestures and attitudes and can determine personality (for example the passivity of Orientals), since wearing a mask, for example changes the attitudes of the wearer. So, the work overall experiments carried out in theatrical shows, seemed sad to Kuzmin, because it consistently impeded that vital interior rapport of the artist with his costume.

This attention to the psychological origins of creativity are also explained in the research on primitive art, to which an entire section of the RAC*h*N, split into different art departments for the work primitive people and artisans was dedicated. N. Lamanova, one of the founders of *Atelier* together with V. Jasvickij, one of the editors of the periodical, was in fact, part of the RAC*h*N's Commission for the study of art in industry. In fact, both N. Lamanova and E. Pribylskaja, in creating their designs, not only used forms of peasant dress and traditional themes of embroidery and lace (no different from the enlightened patrons of the beginning of the century like Princess Maria Teniseva[22] or Elizaveta Mamontova[23]), but directly utilized embroidered pieces and printed scarves as mass-produced elements for domestic designs that were simple to produce.

However, whether it was the creation of an artist, craftsman or a domestic product, the clothing promoted by *Atelier* remained a long way from being mass produced. The work overall, but above all the textiles of the Constructivist artists, were on the contrary, designed from the beginning on the basis of mechanical instruments of production. It was not by chance that Liubov Popova and Varvara Stepanova started to design their new textiles, asking the new 'red' director of the First Factory of Printed Cotton in Moscow if they could become directly involved in the productive process[24]. It seems that the two artists were met with a certain skepticism on the part of the workers, and, in each case, the geometric designs proposed by them were not the metaphoric rationalization of the productive process but a mecchanisation of image which corresponded, in the theatrical field, to the mechanization of movement in bio-mechanics. The differentiated, separate and precise gestures of the assembly line opposed the languid continuous gestures of the dance: the waltz and tango to whose influence the *Atelier* had directly dedicated an article[25].

A rhythm, therefore, different from that theorized by *Atelier*, presided over the non-figurative textiles of the two artists, who in their geometric decorations often used the principles of optical illusion, thereby anticipating optical research in the Sixties. L. Popova, in particular, who often designed her textiles in relation to the shape of the clothes, utilized these same illusionistic principles in order to facilitate the passage from the two-dimensional surface of the material to the three-dimensional volume of the human figure[26].

The intuition of the two Constructivist artists found a logical continuity in the scientific research published at the beginning of the Thirties by the Gossveiprom (State Clothing Industry). This was a series of articles on 'Colour in Clothing'[27] which appeared in the new periodical *The Clothing Industry* and dealt with the rational application of colours in clothing based on extensive and profound research into the theory of colour (not excluding the psychological theories of chromotherapy). As a complement to this, a manual on *Dress design according to the laws of visual perception* (1934)[28] analyzed the theory of the applied shape to clothes. The editor of these texts was Sofija Beljaeva-Eksempljarskaja, a psychologist of perception, who at the age of twenty worked in the Psychological Laboratory of the RAC*h*N, in the section founded by W. Kandinsky in 1921.

In S. Beljaeva-Eksempljarskaja's texts there existed a hiatus between pure theoretical research and the ordinary 'applied' aspect of that research, between an up-to-date gestalt bibliography of European and American articles from specialized periodicals, and the use of Hering laws to whittle down a silhouette, Poggenderff laws to put right cutting errors and the Zollner law to correct physical imperfections. This research radicalized, perhaps unknowingly, the idea of the work overall, as well as the real work overall (it underlined the necessity to emphasize colours for the safety of the worker) and standardized clothing for the technical requirements of production.

The debate on standard dress, so popular in the Soviet Union towards the end of the Twenties, can really refer to those textiles of this exhibition where iconographic themes of propaganda: 'tractors', 'pioneers', '15 years of the Red Army', etc, become a series of pictorial symbols rhythmically repeated and in which statistics are given visual form[29].

The visualization of statistics was one of the themes that was taken up by avant-garde graphics designers (for example El Lisitsky) in the second half of the Twenties and which was complimentary

The role of the meeting point of lines in dress, by S. Beljaeva-Ekzempljarskaja, 'Dress design according to the laws of visual perception', 1934.

The optical illusion of Muller-Lyer applied to a dress, by S. Beljaeva-Ekzempljarskaja 'Dress design according to the laws of visual perception', 1934.

to the research into the standard in all fields. The context of the ideological message therefore became divorced from the quantification in the same way in which the numerous repetitions on textiles of that message became the most conformist reconciliation to the new structure of the mass society in the Thirties.

1. *Atel'e*, n.1, Petrograd, 1923.

2. *Sveinaja promyslennost*, (The Clothing Industry), n.1, Moscow,1929.

3. T. Strizenova, *Avtor kostjuma Aleksandra Exter* (The costume of designer A. Exter), in *Dekorativnoe Iskusstvo SSSR*, n.1, Moscow, 1967, pp.31-34; A. Exter, *Sovremennaja odezda. Prostata i prakticnost v odezde* (Contemporary Dress. Simplicity and Practicality in clothing), in *Krasnaja Niva*, n.21, Moscow, 1923, p.31; A. Exter, *Sovremennaja odezda, ibidem*, n.22, p.28.

4. P.K. Suzdalev, *Vera Ignat'evna Muchina*, Moscow, Iskusstvo, 1981, pp. 45-49.

5. T. Strizenova, *Iz Istorii sovetskogo kostjuma*, Moscow, Sovetskij Chudoznik, 1972.

6. During the Exhibition, the organising Committee of the RAChN also published three issues of a journal *Vedi: Vserossijskaja Vystavka Chudozestvennoj Promyslennosti*, n. 1-3, Moscow, 1923.

7. A.E-r (Exter), *V poiskach novoj odezdy, ibidem*, n. 2, pp. 16-18.

8. A. Exter, *V konstruktivnoj odezde*, in *Atel'e*, n. 1, pp. 4-5.

9. N. Ereinov, *Oblik parizmnki 1923 g.* (The Paris Image in 1923), in *Atelier*, cit., pp.7-8.

10. E. Prybyl'skaja, *Vysivka v nastajascem proisvodstve* (Embroidery in today's factory), in *Atel'e*, cit., pp.7-8.

11. Many unpublished materials concerned with these two workshops are found in the Moscow Central Archives of Art and Literature (CGALI) and in the Russian Academy (then State) of Artistic Science (GAChN), n. 941.

12. On the history of that Academy founded in October 1921, see A.I. Kondrat'ev, *Rossijskaja Akademija Chudozestvennych Nauk*, in *Iskusstvo*, n. 1, Moscow, 1923, pp. 407-499, P.S. Kogan, *Gosudarstvennaja Akademija Chudozestvennych Nauk* in *Pecat i revolijucija*, n.7, Moscow, 1927, pp. 293-299; *GAChN Otcet 1921- 1925*, Moscow, 1926 and the archive cited.

13. *Attestat I-oj stepeni na Vserossijskoj Chudozestvenno-promyslennoj Vystavke, Atel'e Mod*, in *Atel'e*, cit., p.48.

14. *Ot redakcii*, in *Atel'e*, cit., p. 3.

15. *Ibidem*

16. John E. Bowlt, *Abramtsevo and Talashkino*: The Emergence of the Neo-nationalist Style, in *The Silver Age: Russian Art of the Early 20th Century and the World of Art Group*, Newtonville, Oriental Research Partners, 1979.

17. Chapter 7 of S. Serbatov, *Chudoznik v usedsej Rossij*, New York, Cechov, 1955, contains details referring to this show, also see N. Misler, *The neo-Russian revival in the World of Art – from artisanship to design*, in *Mir iskusstva: Figurative literary and musical culture in Russian Symbolism*, Rome, n.k., 1980, pp. 55-64.

18. V. Fon-Meck, *Kostjum i revoljuciija*, in *Atel'e*, cit., pp. 31-32.

19. A. Exter, *V konstruktivnoj odezde*, cit., p. 5.

20. The Choreography Studio of the RAChN was led by Aleksandr I. Larionov and he worked in collaboration with Nina Aleksandrova, the organiser of the 'Rythms Association' at the beginning of the Twenties. Together with photographic and cinema specialists, the Studio organised, from 1925 to 1928, four exhibitions on *The art of movement*. Wide ranging material on this studio and the theories of rhythm are cited in the GAChN of the CGALI. See also A.I. Larionov, *Chudozetvennoe dvizenie* (The artistic movement), in *Teorija i praktika fizkul'tury*, IV Moscow, 1925, pp. 72-82; N.G. Aleksandrova, *O ritmiceskom vospitani* (On rhythmic instruction), Moscow, Narkompros, 1920.

21. M. Kuzmin, *Vlijanie kostjuma na teatral'nye postanovki* (The influence of costume on scenography), in *Atel'e*, cit., pp. 22- 23.

22. M. Teniseva, *Vpecatlenija moej zizny* (Impressions of my life), Paris, Russkoe Istoriko-genelogiceskoe Obscestvo vo Francii, 1933.

23. R. Grover Stuart, *Savva Mamontov and the Mamontov Circle: 1870-1905. Art Patronage and the Rise of Nationalism in Russian Art*, PhD Thesis, unpublished, University of Wisconsin, 1971.

24. A. Abramova, *Odna iz pervych* (One of the first), in *Dekorativnoe Iskusstvo SSSR*, n.9, Moscow, 1963, pp. 19-21.

25. M. Jur'evsakja, *Vlijanie tanca na modu* (The influence of dance on fashion), in *Atel'e*, cit., pp. 10-11.

26. E. Murina, *Tkani Ljubovi Popovoj* (The textiles of Liubov Popova), in *Dekorativnoe Iskusstvo SSSR*, n. 8, Moscow, 1967, pp. 24-27.

27. S. Beljaeva-Ekzemplijarskaja, *Cvet v odezde* (Colour in Clothing), in *Svejnaja promyslennost'*, n. 8/9, Moscow, 1932, pp. 24-36; idem, *Vzaimo dejstve cvetov v odezde* (The reciprocal influence of colours in clothing), ibidem, n. 4/5, n. 6/7, n. 8/9, pp. 42-48, 5-10, 4-13.

28. S. Beljaeva-Ekzemplijarskaja, *Modelirovanie odezdy po sakonam zritel'nogo vosprijatija*, Moscow-Lenningrad, Gizlegprom (State Publications of light industry), 1934.

29. F. Roginskaja, *Sovetskij Tekstil*, Moscow, Izd-vo Akc.O-vo AChR, 1930; I. Jasinkaja, *Sovetskie Tkani, 1920-1930-ch godov*, Lenningrad, Chudeznik RSFSR, 1977.

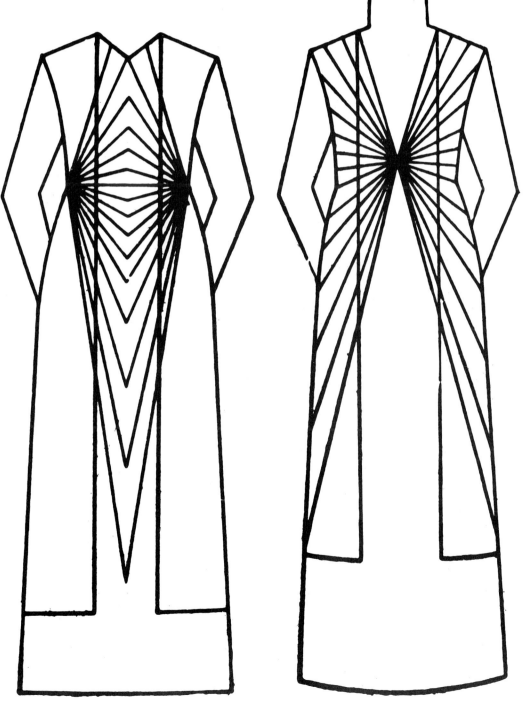

Wundt and Hering's optical illusions applied to dresses by S. Beljaeva-Ekzempljarskaja, 'Dress design according to the laws of visual perception', 1934.

*Photograph of
foundation course
pupils at the
Vkhutemas, before
1926.*

THE VKHUTEMAS
AND THE BAUHAUS:
A COMMON STORY?

Franco Panzini

Many of the artists who worked in textiles during the ten years following the Revolution came from the Vkhutemas[1], an art school in Moscow that was active in the Twenties. The Vkhutemas, together with the contemporary institute of the Weimar Bauhaus in Germany, constituted *par excellence* the places in which the avant-garde European artists conceived and conducted a teaching experiment, a school. Even though the social and political scenario in which the two experiments unfolded are dissimilar, it is however possible to trace a red thread which reflects their respective parallel histories: in the structure of the didactic system, in the evolution of that system during ten years of activity, and in the diaspora that in both cases separated teachers and dispelled ideas.

The scenario that was seen to emerge at the beginning of this century was a Europe where there were more initiatives taking place in the search of a new dimension in art teaching, which leant towards interdisciplinarity, and the marriage of art and industrial production, than there were in the new dimensions of trade called for or in the proposals of associations like the German Werkbund. The war, in a Europe where empires collapsed and new social classes and needs emerged, had determined the future, making clear the requirement for a new type of technician-artist capable of responding to the changed objectives of the market.

So whilst history remembers the Vkhutemas and Bauhaus as being avant-garde, it also remembers the more daring experience of reform which took place in the appointed places of experimentation and production as well as in the transmission of methods of artistic production which were backed up by other experiments in Europe and created specifically in response to the new demands: the craft businesses in the furnishing and clothing sectors who achieved industrial dimensions of production and distribution, the municipalities, the associations, cooperatives and philanthropic home producers[2].

The outcome of both experiences, at the beginning of the Thirties, marked the end of a singular mode, (or rather an unstructured link), between the arts, sciences, and technology, in favour of a renovated priority of construction activity: architecture and design.

The institution of the Vkhutemas, the Muscovite school of applied art, whose name comes from the abbreviation of the words *Vyscie Khudozestvenno-tekhniceskie Masterskie*, Higher State Artistic-Technical Studios, reopened in December 1920. The creation of the school followed a series of previous restructurings in the art education sector which had been carried out in the period immediately following the Revolution.

The most significant had been that of SVOMAS, the free State art studios, instituted in the Autumn of 1918 on the ashes of the Czarist school of art, with the objective of marrying the action of the revolutionary government with the new forms of artistic expression. The artists were young, with different tendencies, and acquired a central role in the organization of the new school that was open to pupils without any requirement of special preliminary instruction and in which that integration between different artistic activities, that was later applied in the Vkhutemas, was put to the test.

The initial didactic structure of the Vkhutemas brought together the regular artistic disciplines with those more typical of design. The school, that counted an average 1500 pupils per year, was organized on a two-year basis (limited to one year after 1926) and was made up of specific departments of painting, sculpture, ceramics, typography, architecture, metalwork, woodwork and textiles. These first two years served as a foundation course which had to act as the basis for the successive artistic specializations, without any concept of hierarchy between the different forms of expression. The course was based on a free approach to materials. Students studied the analytical attitudes and techniques developed by practical experiments in the composition of structure and form, space and volume, dynamic and static structures, with the simplest and most varied materials used in economical ways.

The cultural life of the institution was marked by the exuberance of the teaching environment, which characterized this school in a way particularly respected by the Bauhaus, which, despite the dialectical openness between teachers and students being one of the foundations upon which its teaching was laid, always remained a school for maestros. The Vkhutemas debated the nature and role of art in the new post-revolutionary society, the rapport with the bourgeois artistic tradition and the value of the art object as capable of initiating a new culture. The climate of the school has been well described in an interview that Naum Gabo gave in 1956: 'What is important to know about the school is that it was something absolutely autonomous. It was both a school and a free academy, where not only normal academic teaching of special professions was carried out . . . but general discussions were held and seminars conducted amongst the students on diverse problems where the public could participate and artists not officially in the faculty could speak and give lessons. It had an audience of several thousand students, although this was a changing one due to the civil war and the war with Poland. There was a free exchange between different workshops as well as within the private studios such as my own . . . . During these seminars, as well as during the general meetings, many ideological questions between opposing artists in our abstract group were thrashed out and discarded. These gatherings had a much greater influence on the later development of constructive art than all the teaching.'[3]

The conception of the school's structure was above all influenced by the discussions and resolutions which took place in the organization of the INChUK, the Institute of Artistic Culture, assembled together for the first time in Moscow in March 1920 and active until 1924, which brought together artists who founded a Soviet proprium in 1919. Kandinsky, who had assumed a predominant role in the INChUK heavily influenced the structure of the education programme in the Vkhutemas, proposing, in line with his theories, a school structured as an experimental centre for research and practice and an independent workshop for the arts in accordance with an objective and scientific interplay with art; this idea had for a long time been a trait of his own artistic analyses and of his didactic work. In a report prepared in 1920 for the National Conference on Art Instruction, Kandinsky wrote: 'Two significant processes have recently been realised: a profound observation in every branch of art, a tendency to analyze its own qualities and to understand it's essence and value; together with a process of cohesion between the arts. Analyzing its problems in depth has become a natural phenomenon in which the individual arts observe with interest their neighbouring disciplines, and thus by examining closely each other's methods, they can be helped to resolve their own similar problems'[5].

So at the Vkhutemas the possibility of analyzing artistic expression in it's individual and precise components, and in the inter-dependencies that merge it into a vision of artistic unification and universalist was experimented with. Kandinsky proposed a method of analyzing the means of expression from the point of view of the mental and physical structure of a man who was then repressed even by other pupils, like Ladovsky who in the Vkhutemas applied psycho-technical methods to the approach to architecture and mathematical formulae to spatial combinations.

In 1921, disappointed by the resolute criticism of his action and his theories, Kandinsky left the Soviet Union once and for all, in order to return to Germany where he had served his artistic apprenticeship. In the following year he was called to the Bauhaus, where he first of all directed the studios of picture murals, and where he remained until its winding up in 1933. It is interesting to note that Kandinsky found in the Bauhaus an atmosphere more favourable to receiving his methods of approach to the artistic question, but he nevertheless continued to propagandize, finding a welcome in the European avant-garde magazines[6]. In 1926, evidently remembering the bitter Muscovite debates, he wrote:

'The young artist, in particular the beginner, must be accustomed right from the start to an objective way of thinking, that is a scientific way of thinking. . . He must learn to find his way along through the 'isms', which as a rule do not get to the heart of the matter but concentrate their attention on the ephemeral details . . . However, this simple matter of fact remains completely alien to the leading artistic institutions[7].'

The opposition to Kandinsky had been conducted by the Rodchenko group, developed from 1920 in the INChUK, to which had joined among others, Stepanova and Popova; their aim was the research of a less subjective approach to the artistic question. In 1921 they formed, as is well-known, the work group of Constructivists, with an active and later predominant didactic presence inside the Vkhutemas.

The basic course at the Vkhutemas had a function of wide didactic experimentation, similar to that of the *Vorkurs* developed at the Bauhaus, although perhaps with a greater freedom of participation on the part of the students. The two-year course

started with three sessions and three centres of interest. The graphic centre had Rodchenko among its instructors. The centre of surface and colour studied the optical response of surfaces and their formal characteristics and it was sub-divided into a series of workshops, which were concerned, among other subjects, with pictorial space (under the direction of Vesnin and Popova), the relationship of shapes to light and the construction of mass and space (under the direction of Rodchenko). The third centre, of volume and space, was in its turn sub-divided into two different sections from 1925: the first became a preparatory course for sculpture, and the second related to the properties and composite principles of spatial forms, and introduced students to the rudiments of architecture.

Thus the main courses of the Vkhutemas and Bauhaus also presented a notable similarity in thematic articulation[8]. The discovery strangely can be seen in both schools, standing alongside the regular teaching of artistic institutions, and those of typography and textiles. The former found an explanation linked to the development of new means of information and publicity, together with the need for publication and promotion of the results produced and a sustained theoretical standpoint. For the second sector the justification is more vague and can not be simply traced back to the industrial transformation of textile production and therefore to the birth of textile design. It is perhaps true (and in the case of Bauhaus it is explicit in the testimonies of his women pupils), that the department was created in order to offer a place to what was a true novelty: the presence of women inside the two schools.

The division between the departments set up beforehand the ground for a still greater call for autonomy, as happened for that of architecture, which tried to break away in order to become a faculty in its own right. In 1927, following some wide reforms to the academic structure, the school altered its name to that of *Vkhutein*, shortening the name to High State Art-Technical Institute. The reform carried with it a progressive loss of the links between the various studios and departments which ended up in 1930 with the disintegration of the school into separate and specialized institutes. Something similar also happened in the Bauhaus where, in the final years of activity, a general reorientation towards architecture, design and the

intellectual aspect of technology took place as described in Schllemmer's letter in which she denounced the event, and the survival of the individual disciplines depended purely on how many functions it could carry out.

There was a basic difference which separated the two schools. In the Bauhaus, the much sought rapport with industry, even though in an experimental form, took place, stimulating the alignment of the tendencies of the school with the refinement of the New Objectivity which the new European avant-garde groups were proposing; by contrast in the Vkhutemas, in a still pre-industrial Soviet Union, a rather mythological formula of factory mechanization was evolved without really assessing the innate aesthetic potential of the new materials and productive technology; industry as a fundamental objective almost became an idol, which prepared the way for the return of monumentalism in the Thirties.

This was a danger already predicted in a review in 1923 published by *Izvestia* at an exhibition of industrial design of the Vkhutemas, where we read: 'In the presentation of the subjects there is something which weakens artistic impulse: the scales are too weighed down from the point of view of Mechanization. Thus, for example, in the printing department, the students spend too much time designing machine parts and not enough designing the world about them and studying composition.'[9]

1. For a clear description of the institute, see S. Bojko, *Vkutemas*, in S. Barron and M. Tuchman's, *The avant-garde in Russia*, Los Angeles 1980, pp. 78-83.
2. Even with a vision more geared to design, let us remember, for example, the new course at the Quellinus School in Amsterdam after J.L.M. Lauweriks became director from 1917, or the activity of the Design and Industries Association, formed in 1915 in Great Britain.
3. The step is reported in T. Benton, *The New Objectivity*, Milton Keynes 1975, p.38.
4. On the role of the INKHUK see, among others, S.O. Chan-Magomedov, 'Rodchenko, Stepanova and the artistic organisations' in *Rodchenko, Stepanova. The origins of Constructivism*, Milan, 1984, pp. 20-36, as well as, C. Lodder, 'The Costakis collection: new insights into the Russian avant-garde', in *A.D. Profile*, n. 47/1983, pp. 14-33.
5. The quotation is reported in S. Bojko, *Vkhutemas*, cit., p. 78.
6. See, amoung others, the important study by W. Kandinsky, *Und Einiges uber Syntetische Kunst*, in *The 10*, n. 1/1927, pp. 4-10.

7. W. Kandinskym *Der Wert des theoretischen Unterrichts in der Malerei*, in *Bauhaus*, n. 1/1926.
8. A synoptic picture of the teachings of the Bauhaus in various years is contained in F. Panzini's *Bauhaus*, Venice, 1985, pp. 51-52.
9. Y. Tugenkhold, 'Industrial design at Vkhutemas', the article originally appeared in *Izvestia*, 30 December 1923, and is reproduced in *Art into Production*, Oxford 1984.

COLOUR PLATES

1   2

3

19

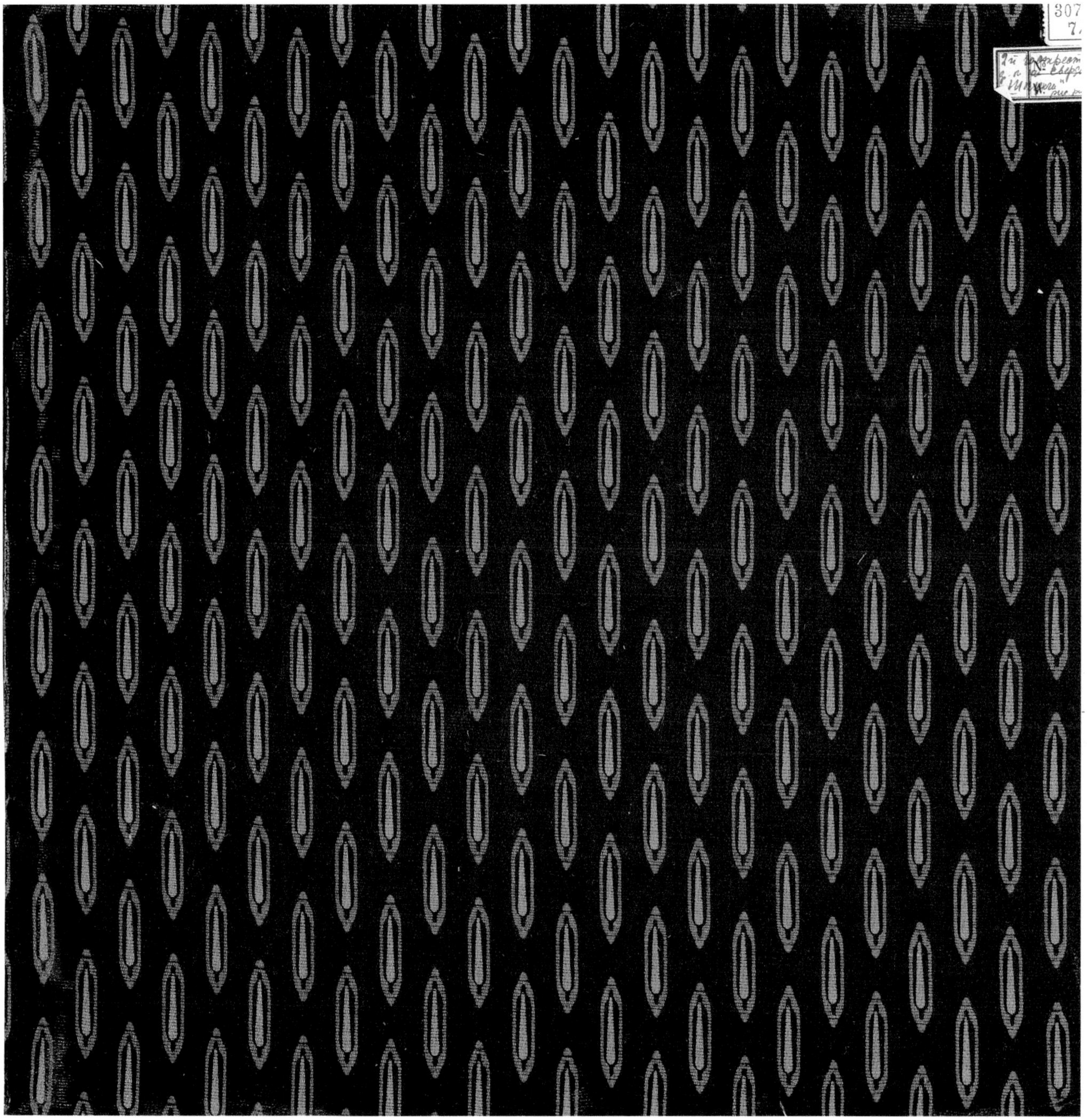

27

28

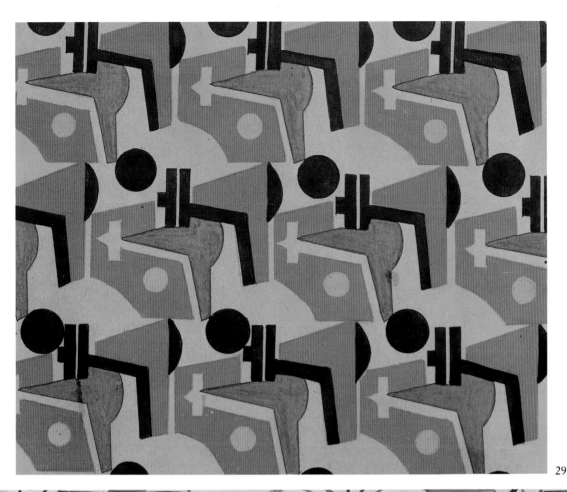

29

30

33

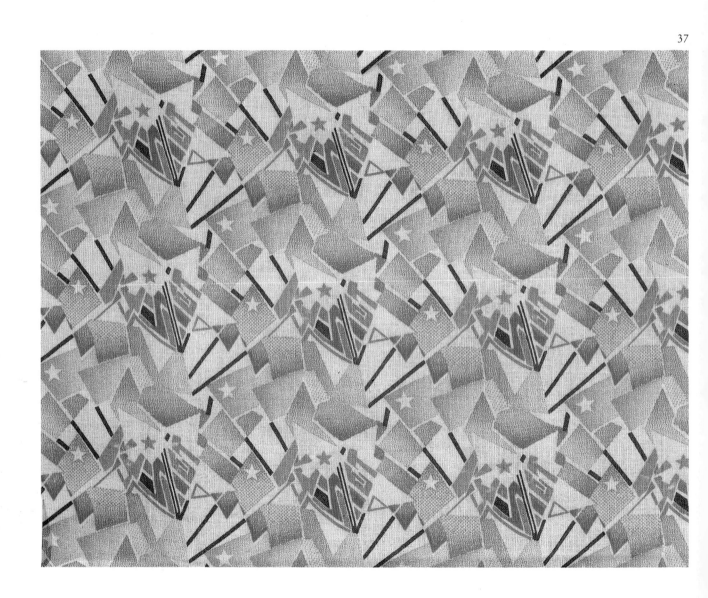

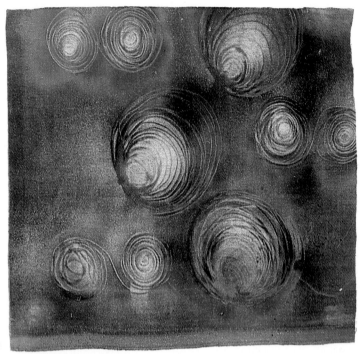

43

44

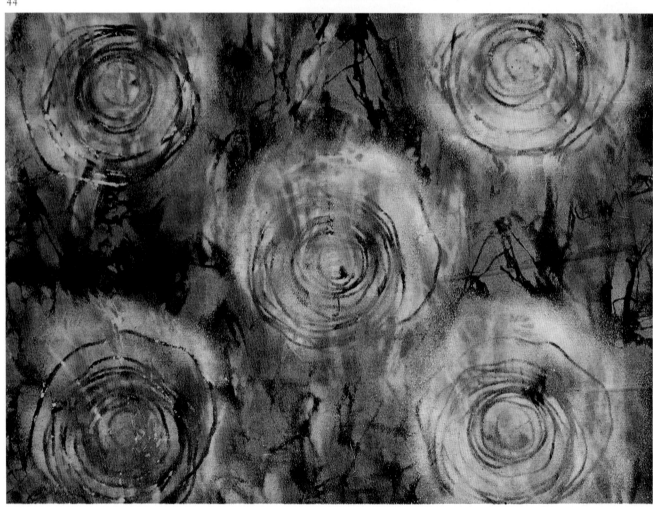

48

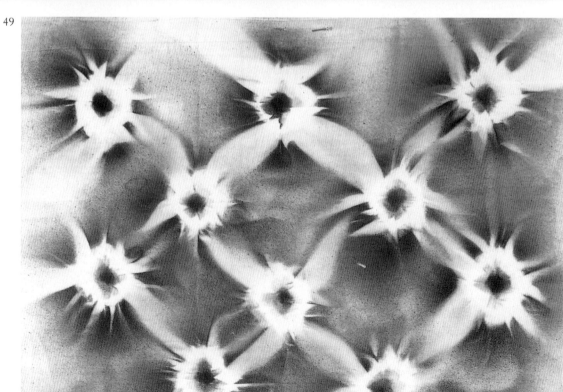

49

50

52   53

55

60

61

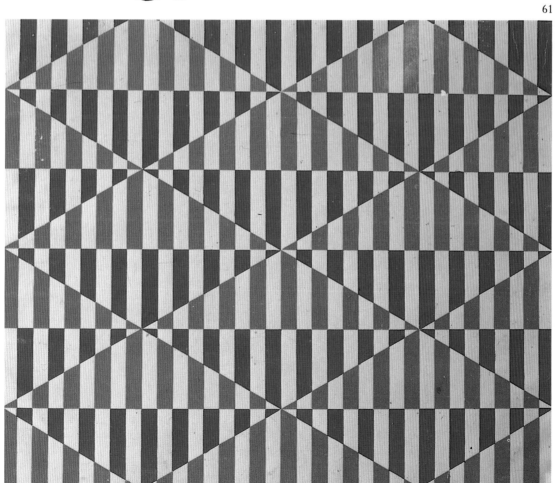

63

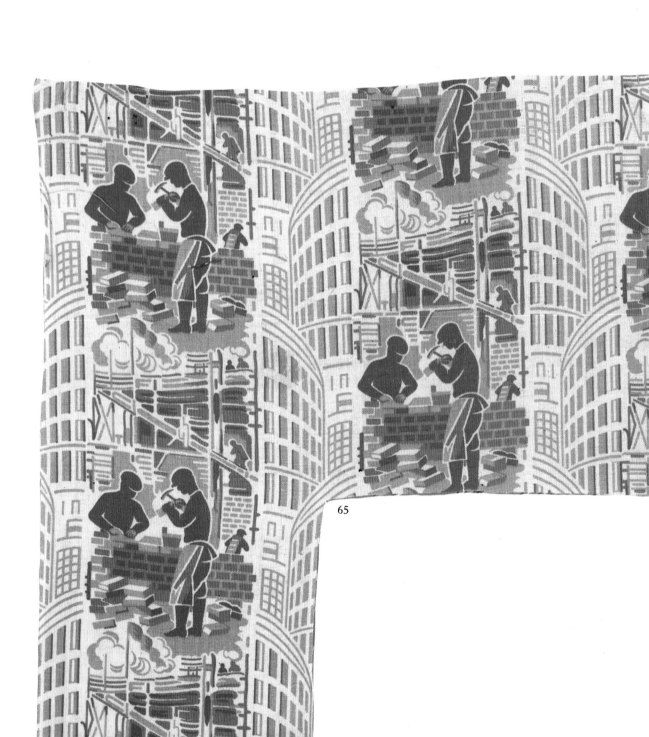

65

66

71

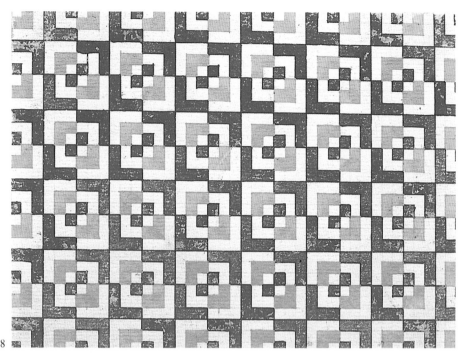

78

79

ПРОЗОДЕЖДА
АКТЕРА
№ 7
А. ПОПОВА 1921

101

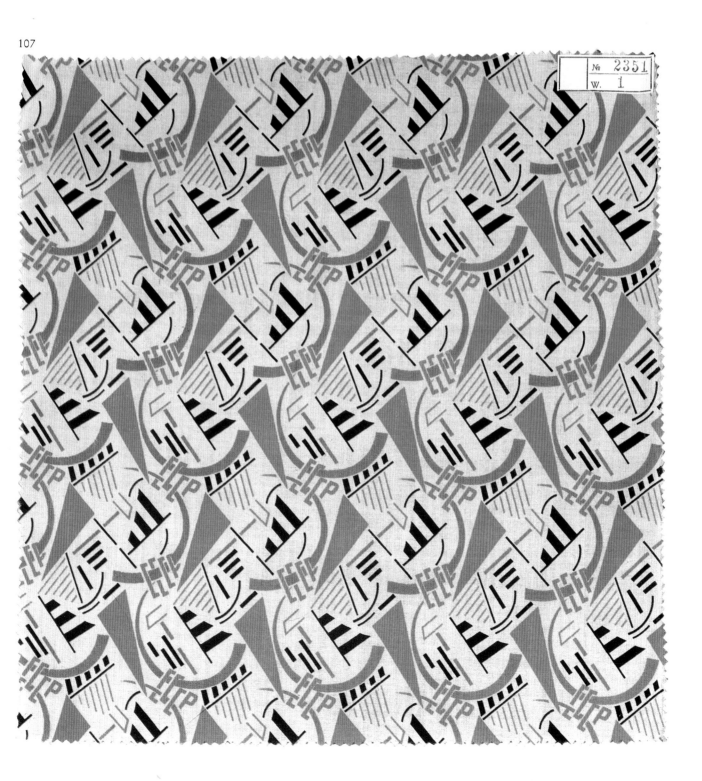

111

САТИН набивной
Стандарт 74 А
Мин. шир. гот. тов. 73 см.

119

123

125

124

146

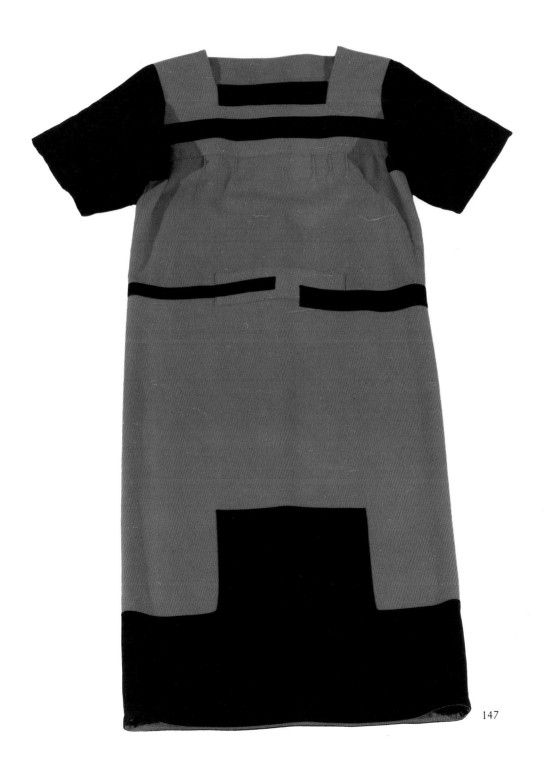

147

144   145   143

120

LIST OF
ILLUSTRATIONS

1. **Nikolai Akimov**
Study for a woman's costume for *Eugraf – the seeker of adventure* by Alexei Fayko
Directed by Boris Suskevich and Serafina Birmann
Set design and costumes by Nikolai Akimov
First performed at the Moscow Arts Theatre 2 on the 15th of September 1926.
Watercolour on paper, 31.4 x 24 cm
Bachrusin Theatre Museum (GCTM), Moscow
See page 60

2. **Nikolai Akimov**
Study for a woman's costume for *Eugraf – the seeker of adventure* by Alexei Fayko
Directed by Boris Suskevich and Serafina Birmann
Set design and costumes by Nikolai Akimov
First performed at the Moscow Arts Theatre 2 on the 15th of September 1926.
Watercolour on paper, 31 x 24 cm
Bachrusin Theatre Museum (GCTM), Moscow
See page 60

3. **Marya Anufrieva**
Water Sports
Indienne cotton, 30 x 29 cm
Manufactured by the IIIrd Internationale Factory, Karabanovo, late 1920s.
Historical Museum (GIM), Moscow
See page 61

4. **Babasev**
Mixed cotton and cashmere cloth on a marine theme, 30 x 53 cm
Manufactured by the *'Krasnaya Roza'* (Red Rose) factory, Ivanovo, late 1920s.
Muchina Design Institute Museum (LUVhPU), Leningrad
See page 62

5. **Babasev**
Harvesters
Indienne cloth, 18 x 17 cm
Manufactured by the *'Krasnaya Roza'* (Red Rose) factory, Ivanovo, 1929.
Strizenova Collection, Moscow.

6. **Zinaida Belevich**
The Children's Demonstration
Clothing material, 25 x 34 cm
Manufactured by the *'V. Sluckaya'* factory, Leningrad, 1930
Muchina Design Institute Museum (LUVhPU), Leningrad

7. **Olga Bogoslovskaya**
Drums
Indienne, 29 x 29 cm
Manufactured by the Zinoviev factory, Ivanovo, 1927
Strizenova Collection, Moscow.
See page 63

8. **Olga Bogoslovskaya**
Small Hammers
Indienne, 24.5 x 22.5 cm
Manufactured by the Zinoviev factory, Ivanovo, 1927
Strizenova Collection, Moscow.

9. **Olga Bogoslovskaya**
Electric Insulators
Indienne, 30.5 x 23.5 cm
Manufactured by the Zinoviev factory, Ivanovo, 1927
Strizenova Collection, Moscow.

10. **Sarra Buncis**
Spinning Yesterday and Today
Clothing material, 26 x 35 cm
Manufactured by the *'V. Sluckaya'* factory, Leningrad, 1930
Muchina Design Institute Museum (LUVhPU), Leningrad

11. **Sarra Buncis**
Tractors
Clothing material in wool, 99 x 74 cm
Manufactured by the *'V. Sluckaya'* factory, Leningrad, 1931
Muchina Design Institute Museum (LUVhPU), Leningrad

5

6

8

9

0

11

12. **Sarra Buncis**
The Ironworks: sketch drawing
Gouache and tempera on paper, 18.5 x 25 cm
1930
Muchina Design Institute Museum (LUVhPU),
Leningrad

13. **Sergei Burylin**
Industry
Woven cotton crepe, 26.5 x 27 cm
Manufactured by the 'Great Manufacturer Iva-
novo-Voznesensk', Ivanovo, 1930
Historical Museum (GIM), Moscow

14. **Sergei Burylin**
Tractors
Indienne, 27 x 27 cm
Manufactured by the 'Great Manufacturer Iva-
novo-Voznesensk', Ivanovo, 1930
Historical Museum (GIM), Moscow
See page 65

15. **Sergei Burylin**
Cotton sample, 27 x 27 cm
Manufactured by the 'Great Manufacturer Iva-
novo-Voznesensk', Ivanovo, 1927
Historical Museum (GIM), Moscow

16. **Sergei Burylin**
The City
Woven cotton, 40 x 27 cm
Manufactured by the 'Great Manufacturer Iva-
novo-Voznesensk', Ivanovo, late 1920s
Strizenova Collection, Moscow.

17. **Sergei Burylin**
After a design by Ivan Biblin
Furnishing indienne, 82 x 63 cm
Manufactured by the 'Great Manufacturer
Ivanovo-Voznesensk', Ivanovo, late 1920s
or early 1930s
Muchina Design Institute Museum (LUVhPU),
Leningrad
See page 66

18. **Oskar Grjun**
Furnishing satin, 65 x 55 cm

Manufactured by the *'Trechgornaya'* factory in
Moscow, late 1920s or early 1930s
Historical Museum (GIM), Moscow
See page 83

19. **Oskar Grjun**
Bobbins
Serge cloth, 40 x 40 cm
Manufactured by the Sverdlov factory in
Moscow, 1928
Russian Museum (GRM), Leningrad
See page 67

20. **Oskar Grjun**
Pioneers
Cotton serge, 27 x 27 cm
Manufactured by the *'Trechgornaya'* factory in
Moscow, late 1920s or early 1930s
Historical Museum (GIM), Moscow

21. **Gurkovskaya**
Turksib (The Turkish Siberian Railway)
Design for an indienne, 20.5 x 15.5 cm
Ivanovo, late 1920s or early 1930s
Strizenova Collection, Moscow.

22. **Gurkovskaya**
Ears of Corn
Woven cotton, 14.7 x 24.6 cm
Ivanovo, 1934
Strizenova Collection, Moscow.

23. **Gurkovskaya**
Autumn Leaves
Woven cotton, 18 x 24 cm
Ivanovo, 1934
Strizenova Collection, Moscow.

24. **Gurkovskaya (?)**
The Fleet
Fabric design, gouache on paper, 18.3 x 14 cm
Ivanovo, 1932
Strizenova Collection, Moscow.
See page 68

25. **Gurkovskaya (?)**
Textile Department

13

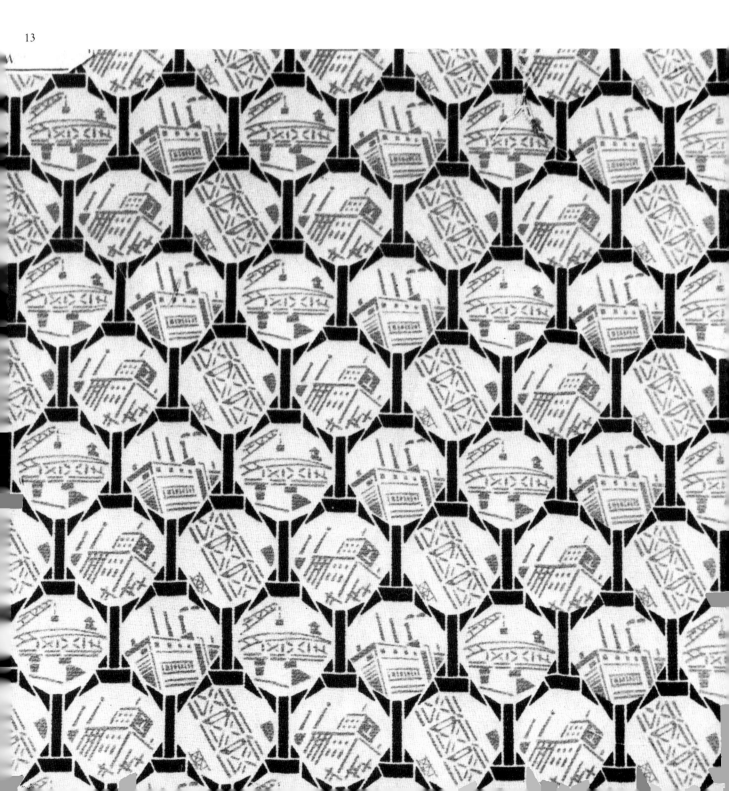

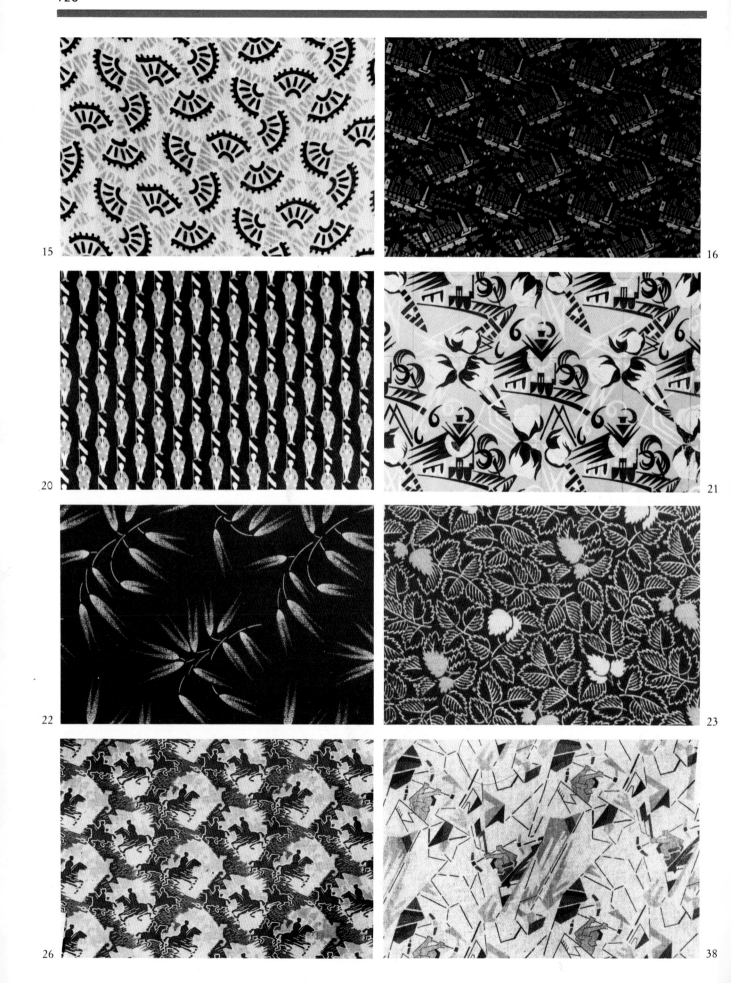

15

16

20

21

22

23

26

38

Fabric design, gouache on paper, 16.2 x 13 cm
Ivanovo, 1932/4
Strizenova Collection, Moscow.
See page 69

26. Demkov
The Buddenyi Cavalry
Indienne for clothing, 30.5 x 60 cm
Manufactured by the '*Piatyi oktabr*' (Fifth of
October) factory, Strunino, Leningrad, 1930
Muchina Design Institute Museum (LUVhPU),
Leningrad

27. Natalya Kiseleva
Design for a shawl
Pencil and watercolour on paper, 37 x 38 cm
1927-29
Russian Museum of Decorative Arts (VMDPiNI),
Moscow
See page 70

28. Natalya Kiseleva
Woven sample
Airbrush on cotton, 55 x 71 cm
1927-29
Russian Museum of Decorative Arts (VMDPiNI),
Moscow
See page 70

29. Natalya Kiseleva
Textile design
Watercolour on paper, 15.5 x 19 cm
1927-29
Russian Museum of Decorative Arts (VMDPiNI),
Moscow
See page 71

30. Natalya Kiseleva
Textile design
Body and watercolour on paper, 17 x 21 cm
1927-29
Russian Museum of Decorative Arts (VMDPiNI),
Moscow
See page 71

31. Alexandra Kolcova-Byckova
Textile design on four sheets
Body and watercolour on paper, 17 x 16 cm
(largest)
1929
Russian Museum of Decorative Arts (VMDPiNI),
Moscow
See page 72

32. Alexandra Kolcova-Byckova
Textile design on four sheets
Body and watercolour on paper, 19 x 11 cm
(largest)
1929
Russian Museum of Decorative Arts (VMDPiNI),
Moscow
See page 73

33. Alexandra Kolcova-Byckova
Textile design
Charcoal and watercolour on paper, 24 x 32 cm
1929
Russian Museum of Decorative Arts (VMDPiNI),
Moscow
See page 74

34. Alexandra Kolcova-Byckova
Textile hanging
Silk, velvet, wool, braid, brocade and cloth,
82 x 106
1929
Russian Museum of Decorative Arts (VMDPiNI),
Moscow
See page 75

35. Vera Lotonina
Fifteen Years of the Red Army
Indienne, 74 x 55
1930s
Russian Museum of Decorative Arts (VMDPiNI),
Moscow
See page 76

36. Vera Lotonina
Airbrushed silk for clothing, 53 x 28 cm
Manufactured by the '*Krasnaya Roza*' (Red
Rose) factory, Moscow, 1930s.

Russian Museum of Decorative Arts (VMDPiNI),
Moscow
See page 77

37. **Lechtman**
Weavers at their machines
Clothing satin, 33 x 80 cm
Manufactured by the 'First Factory of Printed
Cotton', Moscow, 1930
Muchina Design Institute Museum (LUvhPU),
Leningrad
See page 78

38. **Loseva**
The Miner
Woolen clothing fabric, 101 x 75 cm
Manufactured by the 'V. *Sluckaya*' factory, Len-
ingrad, 1930
Muchina Design Institute Museum (LUvhPU),
Leningrad

39. **Loseva**
The Fourteenth Anniversary of the Revolution
Clothing fabric, 101 x 81.5 cm
Manufactured by the 'V. *Sluckaya*' factory, Len-
ingrad, 1930
Muchina Design Institute Museum (LUvhPU),
Leningrad
See page 79

40. **Loseva**
The 16th of May – International Youth Day
Woolen clothing fabric, 88 x 74 cm
Manufactured by the 'V. *Sluckaya*' factory, Len-
ingrad, 1930
Muchina Design Institute Museum (LUvhPU),
Leningrad

41. **Maslov**
New Life in the Countryside
Furnishing indienne, 62.5 x 59.5 cm
Manufactured by the Zinoviev factory, Ivanovo,
1926
Muchina Design Institute Museum (LUvhPU),
Leningrad
See pages 80/81

42. **Raisa Matveeva**
Water Sports
Clothing indienne, 40 x 60 cm
Manufactured by the Zinoviev factory, Ivanovo,
1926
Muchina Design Institute Museum (LUvhPU),
Leningrad

43. **Ludmilla Mayakovskaya**
Shell Shapes
Airbrushed velvet, 22 x 21.5 cm
Before 1927
Mayakovsky Museum, Moscow
See page 82

44. **Ludmilla Mayakovskaya**
Rosebuds
Airbrushed velvet, 35 x 28.6 cm
Before 1927
Mayakovsky Museum, Moscow
See page 82

45. **Ludmilla Mayakovskaya**
Dandelions
Airbrush design on paper, 32 x 51 cm
1920s
Mayakovsky Museum, Moscow

46. **Ludmilla Mayakovskaya**
Design for a scarf
Airbrush on paper, 57 x 57 cm
1920s
Mayakovsky Museum, Moscow
See page 84

47. **Ludmilla Mayakovskaya**
Multicoloured Planets
Airbrush on shot silk, 27.5 x 32.5 cm
Before 1927
Mayakovsky Museum, Moscow
See page 85

48. **Ludmilla Mayakovskaya**
Composition with Cogs
Airbrushed velvet, 65 x 18 cm
Before 1927
Mayakovsky Museum, Moscow
See page 86

40

42

49. **Ludmilla Mayakovskaya**
Networks
Airbrushed indienne, 18 x 26.5 cm
Before 1927
Mayakovsky Museum, Moscow
See page 86

50. **Ludmilla Mayakovskaya**
Lightning
Airbrushed velvet, 22 x 38.5 cm
Before 1927
Mayakovsky Museum, Moscow
See page 87

51. **Ludmilla Mayakovskaya**
Geometrics
Airbrushed shot silk, 54 x 40 cm
Before 1927
Mayakovsky Museum, Moscow

52. **Marya Nazarevskaya**
Red Army Soldiers Help with the Cotton Harvest
Furnishing satin, 53 x 72 cm
Manufactured by the 'First Factory of Printed Cotton', Moscow, 1932
Strizenova Collection, Moscow.
See pages 88/89

53. **Marya Nazarevskaya**
'Likbez' (Literacy for all)
Woven cotton, 15 x 19 cm
Manufactured by the 'First Factory of Printed Cotton', Moscow, late 1920s
Strizenova Collection, Moscow.
See pages 90/91

54. **Marya Nazarevskaya**
Tourism
Satin, 30 x 29 cm
Manufactured by the Alexseev factory, Slisselburg, late 1920s
Historical Museum (GIM), Moscow

55. **Marya Nazarevskaya**
Wedge Forms
Woven cotton, 30 x 29 cm

Manufactured by the Alexseev factory, Slisselburg, late 1929
Historical Museum (GIM), Moscow
See page 92

56. **Marya Nazarevskaya**
The 16th of May – International Youth Day
Indienne, 30 x 29 cm
Manufactured by the IIIrd Internationale Factory, Karabanovo, late 1929.
Historical Museum (GIM), Moscow

57. **Elizaveta Nikitina**
Elements from the Factory
Cotton voile, 29 x 30 cm
Manufactured by the Sverdlov factory, Moscow, 1929
Historical Museum (GIM), Moscow

58. **Elizaveta Nikitina**
Children Dancing
Indienne, 65 x 18 cm
Manufactured by the 'First Factory of Printed Cotton', Moscow, late 1920s
Historical Museum (GIM), Moscow

59. **Ljubov Popova**
Costume Sketch no. 7
Ink, watercolour and collage on paper, 33 x 26 cm
1921
Murina & Sarabjanov Collection, Moscow
See page 101

60. **Ljubov Popova**
Sketch for a woman's costume
Watercolour on paper, 33 x 10 cm
1924
Murina & Sarabjanov Collection, Moscow
See page 93

61. **Ljubov Popova**
Fabric design
Watercolour on paper, 9 x 13 cm
1923/24
Murina & Sarabjanov Collection, Moscow
See page 93

45

51

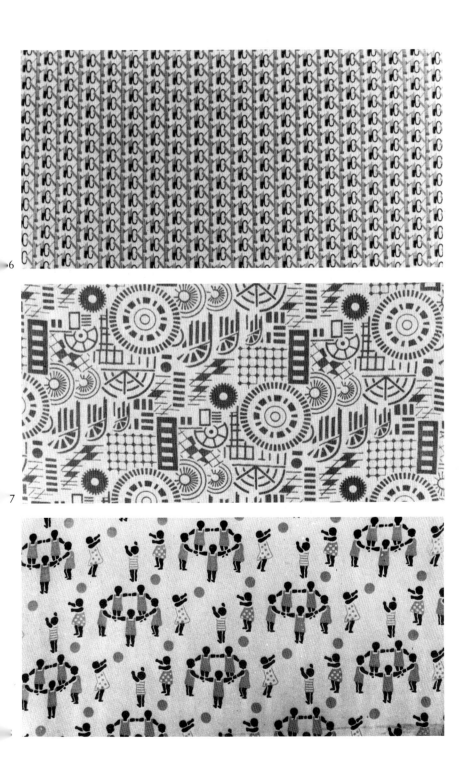

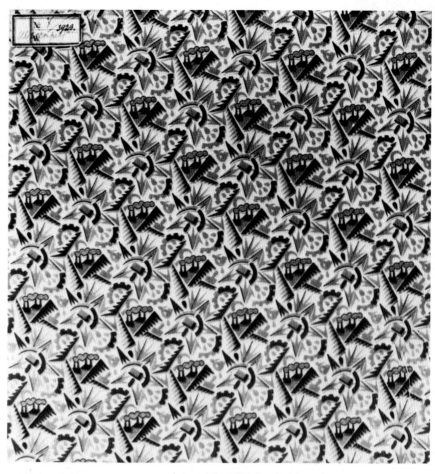

6

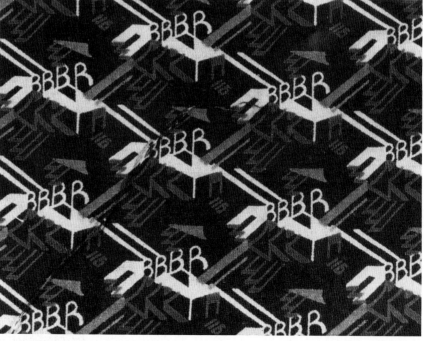

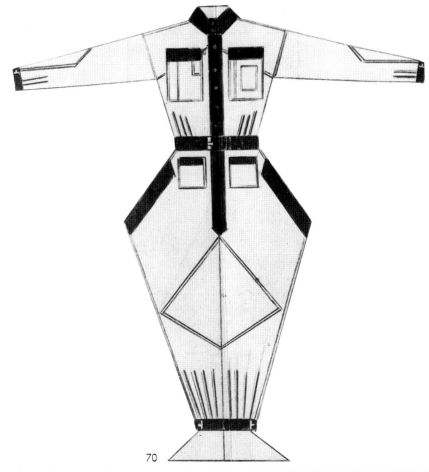

70

72

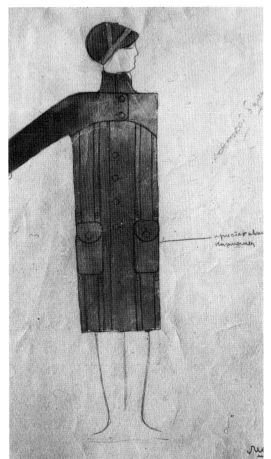

73

62. Darya Preobrazenskaya
Industry
Indienne, 27 x 27 cm
Manufactured by the 'Great Manufacturer Ivanovo-Voznesensk', Ivanovo, 1930
Historical Museum (GIM), Moscow

63. Darya Preobrazenskaya
Water Sports
Flannel, 29 x 29 cm
Manufactured by the 'Trechgornaya' factory, Moscow, late 1920s
Russian Museum (GRM), Leningrad
See pages 94/95

64. Darya Preobrazenskaya
KIM (Communist Youth Organization)
Indienne, 27 x 27 cm
Manufactured by the Zinoviev factory, Ivanovo, 1930
Muchina Design Institute Museum (LUVhPU), Leningrad

65. Darya Preobrazenskaya
Builder's Yards
Indienne, 25 x 16 cm
Manufactured by the 'Great Manufacturer Ivanovo-Voznesensk', Ivanovo, 1931
Strizenova Collection, Moscow.
See page 96

66. Darya Preobrazenskaya
The Eighth of March
Indienne, 25 x 15 cm
Manufactured by the 'Great Manufacturer Ivanovo-Voznesensk', Ivanovo, 1931
Strizenova Collection, Moscow
See page 97

67. Darya Preobrazenskaya
Electrification
Indienne, 24 x 18 cm
Manufactured by the 'Great Manufacturer Ivanovo-Voznesensk', Ivanovo, 1931
Strizenova Collection, Moscow

68. Lya Raycer
Tractors and Corn
Indienne, 27 x 12 cm
1929
Russian Museum of Decorative Arts (VMDPiNI), Moscow

69. Lya Raycer
VKB/P (The Communist Party)
Indienne, 28 x 13 cm
1929
Russian Museum of Decorative Arts (VMDPiNI), Moscow

70. Alexander Rodchenko
Project for a work overall
Coloured paper on paper, 35 x 32 cm
1922
Rodchenko Collection, Moscow

71. Alexander Rodchenko
Fabric design
Coloured inks on paper, 13 x 30 cm
1922
Rodchenko Collection, Moscow
See page 98

72. Alexander Rodchenko
Design for Glebov's *Inga*
Directed by Max Tereskovich
Scenery and costumes by Rodchenko
First performed at the Moscow Revolutionary Theatre, 14th March, 1919.
Design for a woman's costume, 36 x 27 cm
Rodchenko Collection, Moscow

73. Alexander Rodchenko
Design for Glebov's *Inga*
Directed by Max Tereskovich
Scenery and costumes by Rodchenko
First performed at the Moscow Revolutionary Theatre, 14th March, 1919.
Watercolour design for a woman's cape, 36 x 27 cm
Rodchenko Collection, Moscow

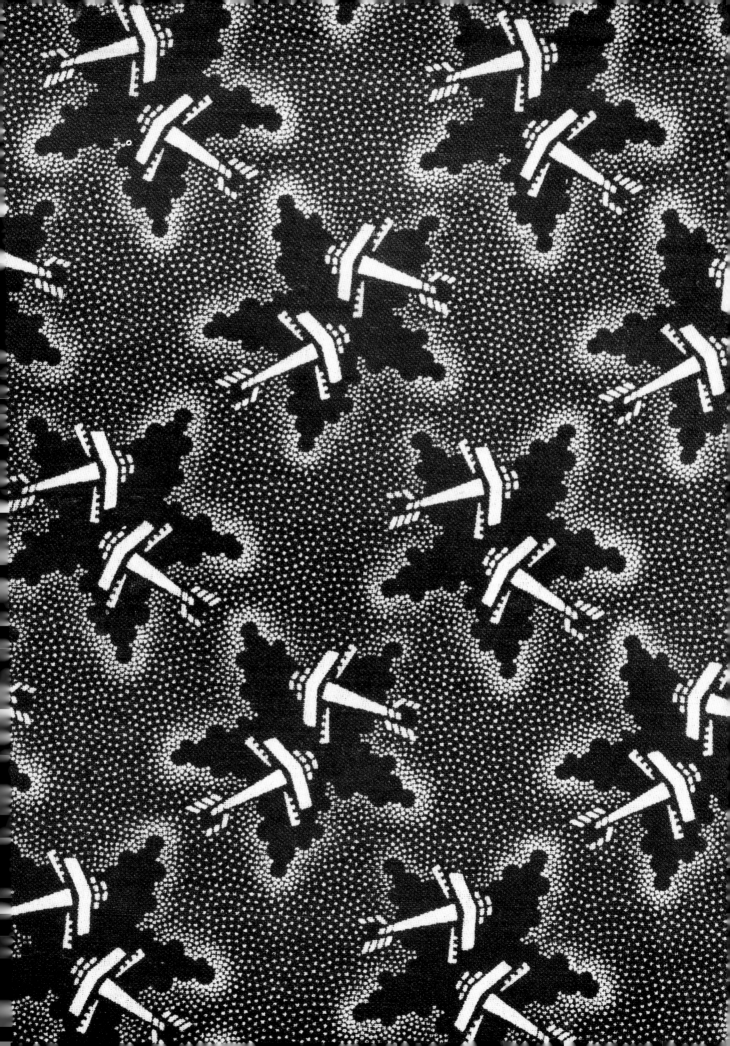

76

77

74. Ljubov Silich
The Harvesters
Indienne, 30 x 20 cm
Ivanovo, late 1920s or early 1930s
Historical Museum (GIM), Moscow
See page 99

75. Solokov
Airplanes and five-pointed stars
Indienne, 26 x 60 cm
Manufactured by the 'Great Manufacturer Iva-
novo-Voznesensk', Ivanovo, 1932
Russian Museum of Decorative Arts (VMDPiNI),
Moscow

76. Varvara Stepanova
Design for costume for a working woman
Ink and gouache on paper, 29 x 22 cm
1924
Rodchenko Collection, Moscow

77. Varvara Stepanova
Design for costume for a working woman
Ink and gouache on paper, 29 x 22 cm
1924
Rodchenko Collection, Moscow

78. Varvara Stepanova
Fabric design
Gouache on paper, 29 x 18 cm
1924
Rodchenko Collection, Moscow
See page 100

79. Varvara Stepanova
Textile design
Ink and gouache on paper, 46 x 55 cm
1924
Rodchenko Collection, Moscow

80. Cacchiani
Air Force Squadron
Part of a scarf
1929
Strizenova Collection, Moscow

81. Anonymous
Wheatsheavess
Appliqué cotton, 27 x 27 cm
Manufactured by the 'Great Manufacturer Iva-
novo-Voznesensk', Ivanovo, late 1920s
Historical Museum (GIM), Moscow
See pages 102/3

82. Anonymous
Airplanes
Indienne, 29 x 20 cm
Manufactured in Ivanovo, early 1930s
Strizenova Collection, Moscow

83. Anonymous
Sailing Boats
Indienne, 50 x 76 cm
Manufactured by the *Krasnaya Roza* (Red
Rose) factory, Moscow, 1930s.
Muchina Design Institute Museum (LUVhPU),
Leningrad

84. Anonymous
Pioneers
Indienne, 52 x 63 cm
Manufactured by the *Krasnaya Roza* (Red
Rose) factory, Moscow, 1930s.
Muchina Design Institute Museum (LUVhPU),
Leningrad

85. Anonymous
Airplanes
Indienne, 42 x 72 cm
Manufactured by the *Krasnaya Roza* (Red
Rose) factory, Moscow, 1930s.
Muchina Design Institute Museum (LUVhPU),
Leningrad

86. Anonymous
Airplanes
Indienne, 32 x 70 cm
Manufactured by the *Krasnaya Roza* (Red
Rose) factory, Moscow, 1930s.
Muchina Design Institute Museum (LUVhPU),
Leningrad

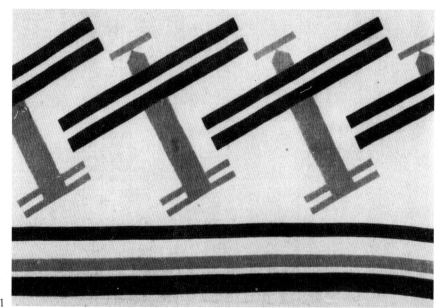

81

82

83

84

85

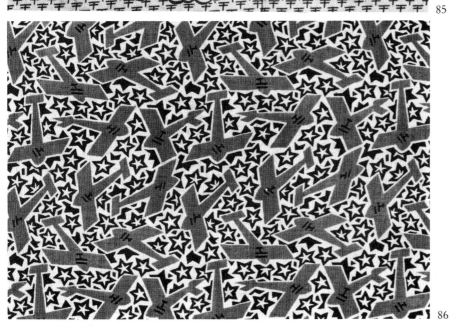

86

87. **Anonymous**
Building Yards
Indienne, 44 x 75 cm
Manufactured by the '*Krasnaya Roza*' (Red Rose) factory, Moscow, 1930s.
Muchina Design Institute Museum (LUVhPU), Leningrad

88. **Anonymous**
Turksib (The Turkish Siberian Railway)
Indienne for furnishing, 100 x 60 cm
Manufactured by the '*Krasnaya Roza*' (Red Rose) factory, Moscow, 1930s.
Muchina Design Institute Museum (LUVhPU), Leningrad
See page 104

89. **Anonymous**
Indienne for furnishing, 37 x 22 cm
Manufactured by the '*Krasnaya Roza*' (Red Rose) factory, Moscow, 1930s.
Muchina Design Institute Museum (LUVhPU), Leningrad

90. **Anonymous**
Tractors for Agriculture
Indienne, 29 x 29 cm
Manufactured by the Sosnev United Factories, Ivanovo, late 1920s.
Historical Museum (GIM), Moscow

91. **Anonymous**
Naval shipyards
Indienne, 29 x 29 cm
Manufactured by the Sosnev United Factories, Ivanovo, late 1920s.
Historical Museum (GIM), Moscow

92. **Anonymous**
Radio sets
Indienne, 13 x 14 cm
Manufactured by the Proletariat Factory, Kalinin, late 1920s.
Historical Museum (GIM), Moscow

93. **Anonymous**
The Red Army on Skis

Indienne, 13 x 14 cm
Manufactured by the '*Piatyi oktabr*' (Fifth of October) factory, Strunino, Leningrad, late 1920s
Historical Museum (GIM), Moscow

94. **Anonymous**
Hammer and Sickle and Gearwheel
Indienne, 29 x 29 cm
Manufactured by the Sverdlov factory, Moscow, late 1920s
Muchina Design Institute Museum (LUVhPU), Leningrad

95. **Anonymous**
Indienne bedlinen, 27 x 60 cm
Manufactured by the Sverdlov factory, Moscow, late 1920s
Muchina Design Institute Museum (LUVhPU), Leningrad

96. **Anonymous**
The Pioneers' Camp
Clothing satin, 23 x 62 cm
Manufactured by the Slisselburg factory, 1930s
Muchina Design Institute Museum (LUVhPU), Leningrad

97. **Anonymous**
Sailing Boats
Clothing fabric, 30 x 60 cm
Manufactured by the Zinoviev factory, Ivanovo, 1939
Muchina Design Institute Museum (LUVhPU), Leningrad

98. **Anonymous**
The Tunnel
Clothing fabric, 24 x 46 cm
Manufactured by the Zinoviev factory, Ivanovo, late 1920s
Muchina Design Institute Museum (LUVhPU), Leningrad

99. **Anonymous**
VKP (The Communist Party)
Clothing fabric in wool, 35 x 25 cm

87

89

90

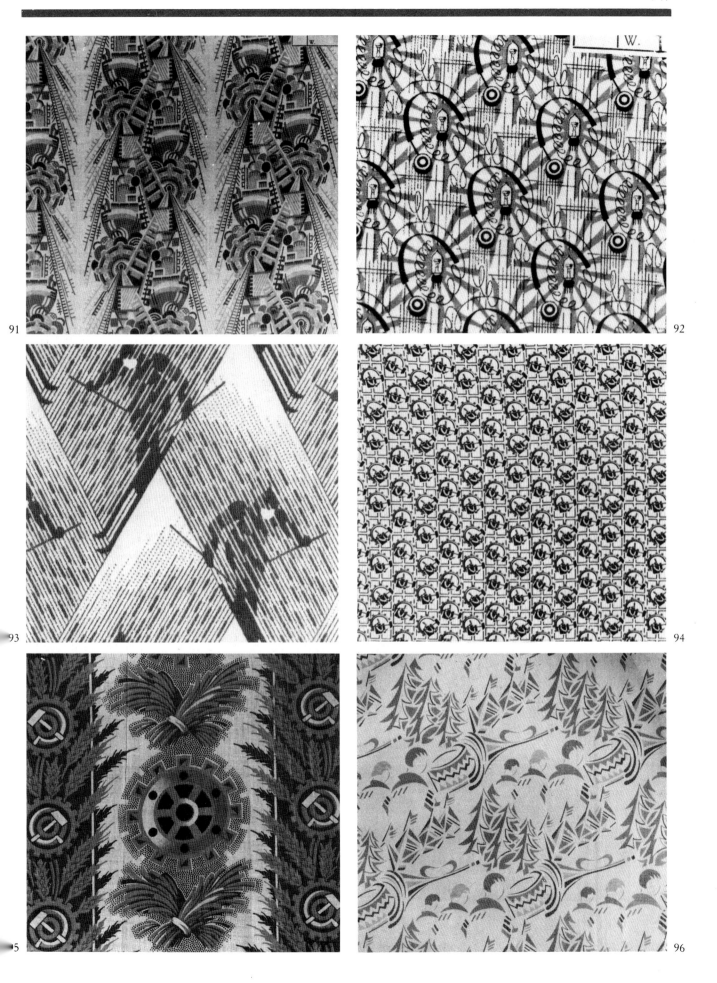

91

92

93

94

95

96

97

98

99

100

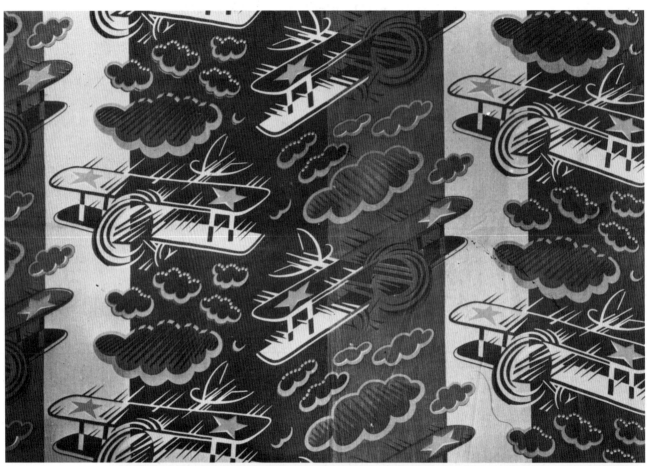

102

106

Manufactured by the 'V. Sluckaya' factory, Leningrad, early 1930s
Muchina Design Institute Museum (LUVhPU), Leningrad

100. **Anonymous**
Long Live Industrialization!
Voile, 29 x 30 cm
Manufactured by the 'V. Sluckaya' factory, Leningrad, late 1930s
Historical Museum (GIM), Moscow

101. **Anonymous**
Sailing Boats
Cotton muslin, 31 x 37 cm
Manufactured by the 'V. Sluckaya' factory, Leningrad, early 1930s
Strizenova Collection, Moscow
See page 105

102. **Anonymous**
Soviet Aviation
Furnishing satin, 56 x 76 cm
Manufactured by the 'First Factory of Printed Cotton', Moscow, 1932
Muchina Design Institute Museum (LUVhPU), Leningrad

103. **Anonymous**
The Red Army
Furnishing satin, 37 x 78 cm
Manufactured by the 'First Factory of Printed Cotton', Moscow, 1930
Muchina Design Institute Museum (LUVhPU), Leningrad
See page 120

104. **Anonymous**
KIM (Communist Youth Organization)
Woven cotton, 37 x 46 cm
Manufactured by the 'First Factory of Printed Cotton', Moscow, early 1930s
Muchina Design Institute Museum (LUVhPU), Leningrad
See page 106

105. **Anonymous**
Socialist Construction
Indienne, 37 x 46 cm
Manufactured by the 'First Factory of Printed Cotton', Moscow, early 1930s
Strizenova Collection, Moscow
See page 121

106. **Anonymous**
Motorcyclists
Furnishing satin, 21 x 8 cm
Manufactured by the 'First Factory of Printed Cotton', Moscow, late 1920s
Strizenova Collection, Moscow

107. **Anonymous**
USSR
Woven cotton, 29 x 30 cm
Manufactured by the 'First Factory of Printed Cotton', Moscow, late 1920s
Historical Museum (GIM), Moscow
See page 107

108. **Anonymous**
Hammer, Anvil and Gearwheel
Indienne, 30 x 29 cm
Manufactured by the 'First Factory of Printed Cotton', Moscow, late 1920s
Historical Museum (GIM), Moscow

109. **Anonymous**
Radio Equipment
Indienne, 29 x 30 cm
Manufactured by the 'First Factory of Printed Cotton', Moscow, 1930
Historical Museum (GIM), Moscow

110. **Anonymous**
Tractors in Column
Indienne, 14 x 15 cm
Manufactured by the 'First Factory of Printed Cotton', Moscow, late 1920s
Historical Museum (GIM), Moscow

111. **Anonymous**
At the Wheel of the Tractor
Indienne, 14 x 15 cm

108

10

110

11

113

1

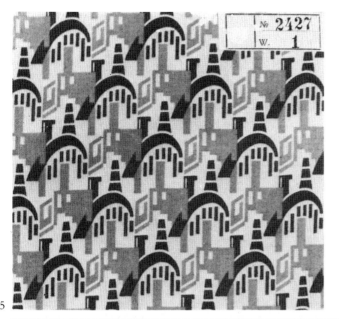

115

116

117

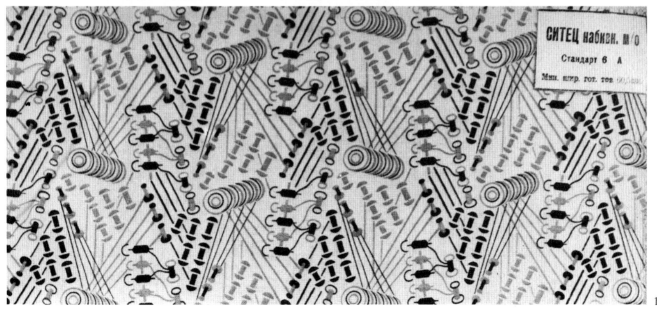

118

120

122

Manufactured by the 'First Factory of Printed
Cotton', Moscow, late 1920s
Historical Museum (GIM), Moscow
See page 110

112. Anonymous
Shuttle and Loom
Indienne, 29 x 29 cm
Manufactured by the 'First Factory of Printed
Cotton', Moscow, late 1920s
Historical Museum (GIM), Moscow

113. Anonymous
Electrification
Indienne, 29 x 30 cm
Manufactured by the 'First Factory of Printed
Cotton', Moscow, late 1920s
Historical Museum (GIM), Moscow

114. Anonymous
The Pioneers' Rally
Indienne, 14 x 15 cm
Manufactured by the 'First Factory of Printed
Cotton', Moscow, late 1920s
Historical Museum (GIM), Moscow

115. Anonymous
The Factories
Satin, 14 x 15 cm
Manufactured by the 'First Factory of Printed
Cotton', Moscow, late 1920s
Historical Museum (GIM), Moscow

116. Anonymous
Cyclists in Column
Satin, 28 x 30 cm
Manufactured by the 'First Factory of Printed
Cotton', Moscow, late 1920s
Historical Museum (GIM), Moscow

117. Anonymous
The Emblems of the USSR
Indienne, 25 x 15 cm
Manufactured by the 'First Factory of Printed
Cotton', Moscow, late 1920s
Historical Museum (GIM), Moscow

118. Anonymous
Textile Machine Details
Indienne, 25 x 15 cm
Manufactured by the 'First Factory of Printed
Cotton', Moscow, late 1920s
Historical Museum (GIM), Moscow

119. Anonymous
The Five Year Plan in Four Years!
Satin, 25 x 15 cm
Manufactured by the 'First Factory of Printed
Cotton', Moscow, late 1920s
Historical Museum (GIM), Moscow
See page 111

120. Anonymous
Industrialization
Satin, 25 x 15 cm
Manufactured by the 'First Factory of Printed
Cotton', Moscow, late 1920s
Historical Museum (GIM), Moscow

121. Anonymous
The Demonstration
Satin, 27 x 27 cm
Manufactured by the 'First Factory of Printed
Cotton', Moscow, late 1920s
Historical Museum (GIM), Moscow

122. Anonymous
The Red Army Parade
Indienne, 24 x 73 cm
Manufactured by the 'Trechgornaya' factory,
Moscow, 1930
Historical Museum (GIM), Moscow

123. Anonymous
The Milky Way
Two pieces of crepe de Chine, 16 x 10
Manufactured at the 'Krasnaya Roza' (Red Rose)
Silkworks, Moscow, early 1930s
Strizenova Collection, Moscow
See page 112

124. Anonymous
Floral Motifs
Two pieces of crepe de Chine, 16 x 10

127

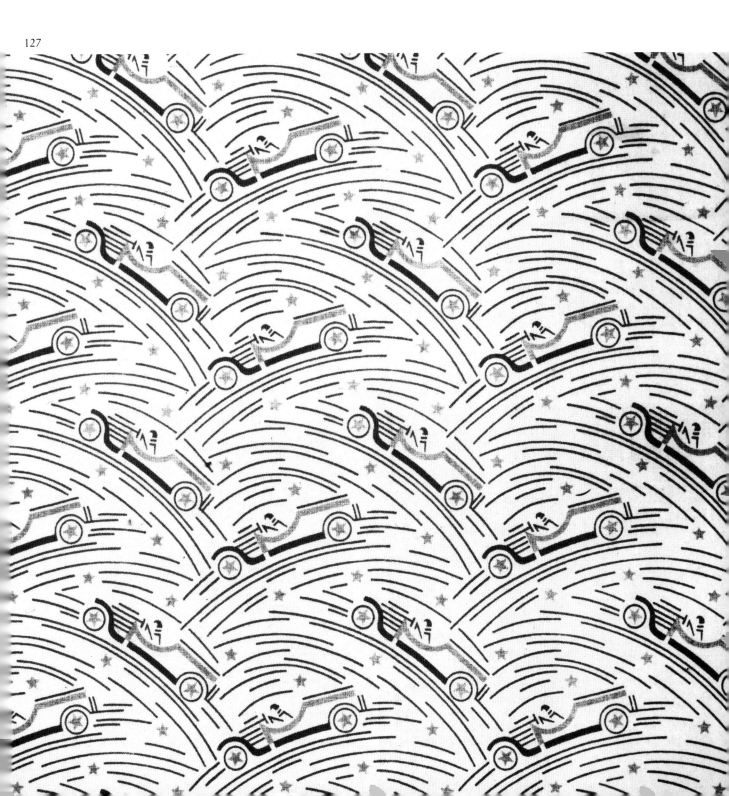

128

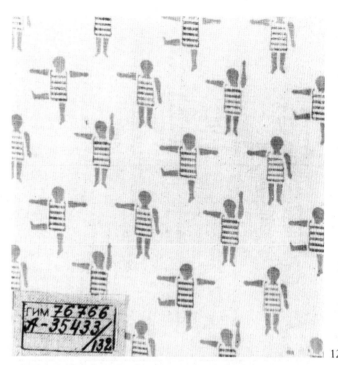

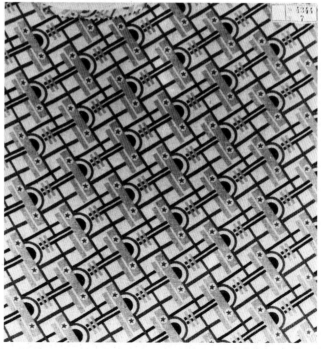

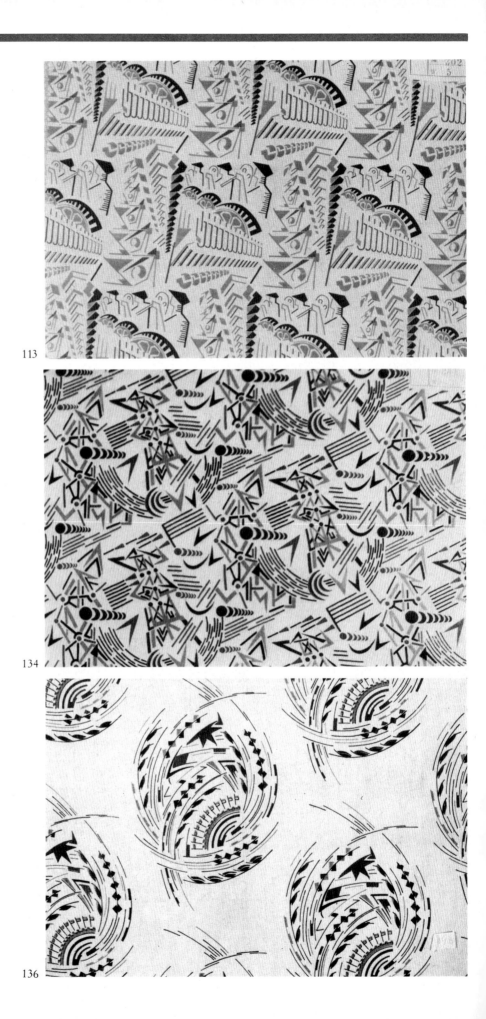

113

134

136

CTK-1108
3

Manufactured at the 'Krasnaya Roza' (Red Rose)
Silkworks, Moscow, early 1930s
Strizenova Collection, Moscow
See page 114

125. Anonymous
White Flowers on a Dark Background
Three pieces of crepe de Chine, 16 x 10
Manufactured at the 'Krasnaya Roza' (Red Rose)
Silkworks, Moscow, early 1930s
Strizenova Collection, Moscow
See page 113

126. Anonymous
Red Flower on Green Background
Crepe de Chine, 16 x 10
Manufactured at the 'Krasnaya Roza' (Red Rose)
Silkworks, Moscow, early 1930s
Strizenova Collection, Moscow
See page 114

127. Anonymous
The Joy of Driving
Indienne, 33 x 60 cm
Manufactured by the 'Second Factory of Printed
Cotton', Serpuchov, 1930
Muchina Design Institute Museum (LUVhPU),
Leningrad

128. Anonymous
The Red Fleet
Satin, 30 x 30 cm
Manufactured by the 'Second Factory of Printed
Cotton', Serpuchov, 1930
Historical Museum (GIM), Moscow

129. Anonymous
Gymnastics
Indienne, 14 x 13 cm
Manufactured by the 'Second Factory of Printed
Cotton', Serpuchov, late 1920s
Historical Museum (GIM), Moscow

130. Anonymous
The Fleet
Indienne, 29 x 29 cm

Manufactured by the 'Second Factory of Printed
Cotton', Serpuchov, late 1920s
Historical Museum (GIM), Moscow

131. Anonymous
Our Air Force
Indienne, 28 x 29 cm
Manufactured by the 'Second Factory of Printed
Cotton', Serpuchov, late 1920s
Historical Museum (GIM), Moscow

132. Anonymous
Airplanes
Indienne, 28 x 29 cm
Manufactured by the 'Second Factory of Printed
Cotton', Serpuchov, late 1920s
Historical Museum (GIM), Moscow

133. Anonymous
The Production Line
Satin, 30 x 29 cm
Manufactured by the Alexseev factory, Slissen-
berg, late 1920s
Historical Museum (GIM), Moscow

134. Anonymous
Electric Transmission Lines
Indienne, 30 x 29 cm
Manufactured by the Alexseev factory, Slissen-
berg, late 1920s
Historical Museum (GIM), Moscow

135. Anonymous
Tugboat and Barge
Satin, 30 x 29 cm
Manufactured by the Alexseev factory, Slissen-
berg, late 1920s
Historical Museum (GIM), Moscow
See page 115

136. Anonymous
Clothing material, 36 x 38 cm
Manufactured by the Alexseev factory, Slissen-
berg, 1930
Muchina Design Institute Museum (LUVhPU),
Leningrad

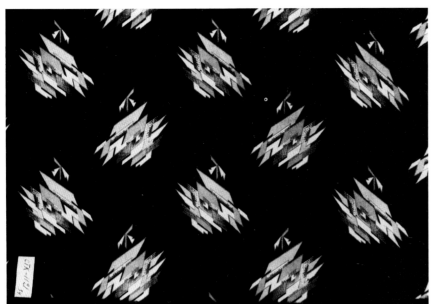

138

139

140

137. **Anonymous**
The News Vendor
Wool, 37 x 59 cm
Manufactured by the Alexseev factory, Slissen-
berg, 1930
Muchina Design Institute Museum (LUvhPU),
Leningrad

138. **Anonymous**
Clothing marquisette, 31 x 86 cm
Manufactured by the Alexseev factory, Slissen-
berg, late 1920s
Muchina Design Institute Museum (LUvhPU),
Leningrad

139. **Anonymous**
Pioneers
Clothing fabric, 31 x 60 cm
Manufacturer unknown, late 1920s
Muchina Design Institute Museum (LUvhPU),
Leningrad

140. **Anonymous**
Clothing fabric, 51 x 77 cm
Manufacturer unknown, late 1920s
Muchina Design Institute Museum (LUvhPU),
Leningrad

141. **Anonymous**
Gearwheels
Clothing cotton, 27 x 26 cm
Manufacturer unknown, late 1920s
Historical Museum (GIM), Moscow
See page 119

142. **Anonymous**
Driving Belts
Woven cotton, 32 x 24 cm
Manufacturer unknown, late 1920s
Strizenova Collection, Moscow

143. **Nadezda Lamanova**
Reproduction of a costume design from 1924
Made by E. Chudyakova from the original
drawings, 1984
USSR Ministry of Culture
See page 118

144. **Ljubov Popova**
*Reproduction of an elegant costume design from
1923/4*
Made by E. Chudyakova from the original
drawings, 1984
USSR Ministry of Culture
See page 118

145. **Varvara Stepanova**
Reproduction of a sports overall from 1923
Made by E. Chudyakova from the original
drawings, 1984
USSR Ministry of Culture
See page 118

146. **Vladimir Tatlin**
*Reproduction of a man's working overall from
1923*
Made from original photographs, 1984
USSR Ministry of Culture
See page 116

147. **Alexandra Exter**
Reproduction of a costume design from 1924
Made by E. Hoffmann-Kenige from the original
drawings, 1979
Russian Museum (GRM), Leningrad
See page 117

142

140

MANIFESTOES AND ARTICLES

ORGANISATIONAL PLAN FOR A WORKSHOP OF CONTEMPORARY COSTUME, 1919

N. Lamanova

The aim and topics of study are:

a) to give artistic value to the industrial production of clothing
b) to make clothing design correspond to our modern way of life and its demands
c) to create artists-instructors of costume design for professional schools, for the theatre and the sewing industry
d) to create 'cadres' of highly qualified producer-craftsmen industrialists

The work programme of the studio will include all related sectors of clothing and connected disciplines.

A. THE FOUNDATION COURSE IN COSTUME DESIGN, BASED ON THE INTEGRATION OF THEORY AND PRACTICE, IS DIVIDED INTO TWO PARTS

1. *Conceiving the garment*
a) the adaptation to the human figure and the suitability of different types of clothing for the individual
b) measurements and form: the study of the figure
c) the design of the garment in geometric shapes as a method of finding a practical solution to a given problem
d) material in relation to shape and purpose
e) colour
f) decoration
g) the function of clothing in everyday life

2. *Making up the garment*
a) the sketch of the garment: creation of a plan
b) the combination of different fabrics (techniques)
c) sewing techniques
d) decorative themes (various types of embellishment)
e) the making up of the garment

B. AUXILIARY DISCIPLINES

a) anatomical proportions
b) hygiene
c) the history of costume (civilian, theatrical and other forms of costume)
d) folk art, its history and techniques (the importance of the Russian peasantry and foreign general design as a primary source of decorative art in it's various manifestations) . . .

The workshop will also study the following:
a) ways of simplifying clothes making simplicity the characteristic of the working-man's clothes in contrast to the clothes of the bourgeoisie
b) the dynamics of contemporary costume
c) the practicality of contemporary clothing (working clothes, everyday wear, smart clothes, sportswear, professional clothes, evening wear and headgear, etc)

Such a course, would not however be complete if it were confined to the industrial section. As it is not just a question of setting up an ordinary workshop or school but a matter of working out a concept and actual methods. It is essential to compliment this part of the programme with a section of theoretical character, which must function as the artistic and cultural education part of the plan. The work should lead to an artistic approach to daily life and in particular to costume in its various forms. Alongside this, problems of practical utility, simplicity and harmony as well as material improvement and evolution of costume must also be studied . . .

ON THE STRUCTURE OF DRESS

A. Exter

Every manufactured article is subject to the laws imposed on it by the material it is made of. When choosing a fabric in order to make a given shape out of it, it is essential to retain its consistency, elasticity, width and colour. Coarse wool, for example, requires a style comprising a rectangular cut, or at least a basic construction of straight corners, without any additional vertical rhythm of tucks, mainly because the fabric adapts badly to folding; in this way we avoid any distortion of the material. Soft wide fabrics (wool or silk appropriately treated) allows for the creation of a more complex and varied silhouette, congruous with more distinctive rhythms. A narrow fabric logically calls for a vertical and close-fitting shape, but the substitution of width for length, can be made up by the use of pleats or vents which is extremely comfortable.

The use of basic materials generates rigour and a clear and simple structure. Materials that give, for example any type of silk, thanks to their special properties, can make it possible to create garments for movement (eg. for dance) and to devise more complicated shapes (circles, polygons). This type of costume, 'constructed' on the dynamic movement of the body, must itself be 'mobile' in its components. A narrower fabric is restricted to a more balanced form (square, triangle, etc) and is associated with slower movements (eg. walking or running).

Shape is inseparable from colour. When studying the look of a garment made in a single colour, and in an elementary geometric shape, we note that the said shape requires the addition of a complementary colour, while a more complicated shape needs tonalism. If we compare two identical squares, one white and one black, the black one appears smaller and more lightweight than the white (according to the theory of colours). For this reason, in order to balance two garments of these colours, it is necessary to make the black shape more complicated. Research into a new type of clothing conforms to the order of the day and, since the working classes make up the majority of the population, clothing must be adapted to suit the workers, and the work which they are carrying out. The overcoat must not be too narrow, since it would impair movement, as would too big a hat or a close-fitting skirt. Contemporary clothing must respond to the requirements of our lives and take into account their diversities. The emphasis must be placed on chromatic intensity, it must characterize Russian folk costume and reject Western European designs and must not be the least bit similar to any other ideology. Work clothes have not yet been completely refined. The style of clothing stems from the conditions of life: work and free time. It is essential to change clothing so it is economic and justifiable, and just as important, it must be both psychologically pleasing and hygienic. Research into the making of the 'prozodezda' (work overall) or mass produced clothing, must be based on extremely simple geometric shapes and complementary colours, which take into account the shape of garments destined for mass production as well as more varied styles. Clothing destined for physical work derives it's movement from the conditions of work and from movements of the body, and must be structured in harmony with the proportions of the human body. The majority of mass-produced articles suffer from a lack of correct proportions and as such, are uncomfortable. For manual workers or those who, in contrast, do not carry out physical work, but who are seated all day at a desk, the superior garment must be adapted to the relevant occupation. This is the theoretical approach to the 'prozodezda' and mass-produced clothes. Totally different types of basic ideas have to apply in the production of individual costume. In this case, representing any typical human categories, getting the right fit, defining the character, and choosing the shape and colour of the garment according to the work for which it is worn, is indispensable. Meanwhile making clothing durable is both the work of the artist and the technician. It is the artist's job to unveil the new shape associated with contemporary man, to find new starting-points for the contemporary clothing, to create expressive styles relevant to the individual garment, to individualize colour and shape, to choose the garments components and 'make it up', and to stabilize the rhythms in accordance with the silhouette of the garment and the dynamism of the human body. A technician, who understands clearly the language of the artist, can translate all this scientific work into reality: the specific role of the technician is of primary importance and is indispensable for the production of a garment. Only with this understanding between the artist and the technician is it possible to resolve the problem of dress.

A. Exter
Atel'e, no. 1, 1923.

RUSSIAN FASHION

N. Lamanova

One of the most fascinating problems of contemporary costume design is how to use and adapt the style and character of folk costume to our everyday clothing. The versatility of folk costume, rooted as it is in popular tradition and inventiveness, can give us both ideological and practical ideas, for our new town. The basic styles of folk-costume are sensible. Therefore, if we take as an example the women's folk-dress of the Kiev province, we see that it consists of a '*skita*' (a type of long jacket), a '*plachta*' - or smock - (a type of skirt) and a blouse with embroidered sleeves and hem. Folk costumes of this kind are, in their own way, work clothes, devised for hard physical work, and can easily be adapted from winter to summer wear; and with the addition of a few trifling accessories such as beads, garlands or a lively coloured apron can also be worn on special occasions. From this type of clothing, linked to actual living and working conditions and which belong to a particular setting based on a feeling for the physical characteristics of the Russian frame, it is easy to design town clothes, that take into account the practicality and colours of the traditional folk-dress. Combining the lively picturesqueness of folk costume with modern techniques of mass production, we achieve a type of clothing that responds to the needs dictated by our contemporary life.

TODAY'S FASHION IS THE WORKER'S OVERALL

V. Stepanova

Fashion which psychologically reflects the '*byt*', that is custom and aesthetic taste, is giving way to programmed clothing, produced in order to suit the work which the wearer is carrying out in different sectors or for a precise social action, as well as clothing which one can not only wear to work, but also elsewhere and which has no independent value and is not an 'artistic product'. The most important thing has become the manufacture (the working of the material), that is the 'realization' of clothing. It is not enough to provide intelligent designs, they need to be made on the production line and given a practical demonstration at work; only then will it be possible to have a clear image of them. Shop windows, containing wax manikins wearing various designs, are only a aesthetic survival. Today's clothing must be seen 'in action', outside of this it is unimaginable, just as any machine is absurd outside of its own work. All decorative detail is abolished with the following slogan: 'The comfort and practicality of clothing must be linked to a specific practical function'. Not only is a mass control on what clothes are worn necessary but clothing must also pass on from being the product of an artisan to that of industrial mass-production. Thus clothing looses its 'ideological' meaning and becomes an aspect of cultural reality. The fact that the evolution of clothing is tied to industrial development, is beyond doubt. Only today, given the far reaching achievements of technology and industry, clothes for pilots and chauffeurs, protective overalls for workers, footballer's boots and military raincoats and jackets have now been produced. In establishing contemporary clothing, one needs to follow it through from the design stage to the material production, where, taking into account the specific nature of the work for which it is intended, one stipulates a particular way of cutting. It is even necessary to substitute aesthetic elements with the production process for sewing the same thing. I'll explain more clearly: one must not sew decorations on the garment, but the same stitching, necessary after the cutting, gives it shape. The stitching of the garment, its buttoning, etc, needs to be laid bear. Nowadays there are no longer unrefined artisanal stitches: the seaming of the sewing machine industrializes tailoring and deprives it of it's secrets, if not of the fascination of the individual-manual work of the tailor. Moreover, the shape, that is the whole exterior look of the garment, today looses all arbitrariness because it is determined by the demands of the job that is predestined for and by the material it is made from. Contemporary clothing is the work overall (prozodezda), that is work clothes that distinguish themselves according to the profession and production. This makes clothing autonomous and at the same time gives it a particular tone. For example, workers clothes must correspond to general rules of cutting: to protect the worker from being wounded by the machine with which he is working. Above all, depending on the nature of production and whether the wearer is a typographer, the driver of a locomotive or a metal- worker in a factory, individual details are introduced, in the choice of material and in the specific nature of the cut, leaving the general design unchanged. With regard to clothing for an engineer-constructor, the general characteristic is the presence of a large quantity of pockets; but this is related to the size and type of instruments that he uses. The shape, size and distribution of pockets depends on whether the workers are working within the wood, weaving, aeroplane, construction or metal-work sectors. A particular place among mass-produced clothes is occupied by the special dress (*specodezda*), which has specific requirements and carries certain equipment. Garments of this type are those of surgeons, pilots, workers who work in factories where acid products are produced, firemen and members of polar expeditions, etc. The sports sector is subject to all the fundamental demands of the '*prozodezda*' and changes appearance according to the sport: football, snow sports, rowing, boxing and athletics. A particular characteristic of sports attire is the necessary inclusion of precise symbols (emblems, shape, colour of the uniform etc.) which distinguish members of one team from another. The colour of sports attire is one of the most important factors, inasmuch as the sporting competitions take place in large areas and in front of a public crowd. To distinguish the participants from a great distance by the cut of the uniform is for the spectator almost impossible, and also when playing in a competition it is much easier to recognize one's own team member by the colour of his uniform. Sports attire must be produced in various colour combinations. The fundamental principle that determines the cut of sports attire for all sports is the following: maximum practicality and simplicity and easy wearability. In this issue of *Lef* we present three types of uniforms for football teams: 1) a uniform of three colours (red, black and grey) with a red star on the chest; 2) a uniform of only one colour (red) in jersey, with a large badge on the chest; 3) a striped uniform of two colours (red and white) without badges. The style of the uniform is a plain shirt with straight sleeves and shorts. The women's uniform for basketball has a black stripe on the chest, and stripes on the skirt which make it appear bell-shaped, etc. Much attention has been given to the simplicity and liveliness of the colour combination. The practical characteristic of the sports uniform is imposed by the simplicity and freedom of movement, in this case because there are neither buttons nor a cut which limits movement.

'Varst' (V. Stepanova) in *Lef*, 1923, 2, pp. 65-68

FROM PAINTING CANVAS TO PRINTING CLOTH

O. Brik

Propaganda for an art of production is destined for success. It is obvious that artistic culture is not just confined to the exhibits displayed in shows and museums, and in particular, painting is not just 'pictures', but all artistic production is part of the everyday reality. *Indienne* cloth is as much a product of artistic culture as the picture, and it would be wrong to distinguish between them in any way whatsoever. What is more, we became even more convinced that the picture is dying, from the moment it was indissolubly associated with the capitalist system and its cultural ideology, and since the artist focused his attention on working with indienne which subsequently revealed itself as being the high point of artistic work.

In fact our cultural creation is based entirely on what is actually achieved. We can not imagine a cultural activity that did not pursue some sort of well defined practical aim. The concepts of 'pure science', 'pure art', 'truth and priceless beauty' are strange to us. We are practical and here lies the crux of our cultural believe. In such a belief easel painting can have no place, because its strength and its significance lie in its extra-usefulness, and it does not serve any purpose other than to give joy and enhance the view. Every attempt to turn an easel painting into an 'agit-picture' has been in vain. This has very little to do with a lack of artistic talent, it is due more to the impossibility of such a thing. The easel painting is created in order to last for years or even centuries. But what propaganda theme is able to resist time? Which agit-picture does not age with the passing of months? And if the theme of an agit-picture ages, what then remains in it? With a theme whose efficacy becomes limited with time, it is not possible to use the same procedures as one would adopt for a work intended to last. A mayfly does not live forever. This is why the agit-picture can not compete with a propaganda manifesto, and why there are no beautiful agit-pictures. The 'purists' of easel painting catch up with the creators of 'agit-pictures' when they abandon propaganda themes. They understand that by competing, easel painting is destined to a sure death and as such, loses its fundamental value, i.e. its 'atemporal' and 'extra-useful' significance, and thus the poster wins. So they make desperate attempts to salvage it in another way: they look for ways to convince us that easel painting, in its purely formal significance, is of enormous cultural value and that without it artistic culture is totally inconceivable. They guarantee that, if they do not carry out easel painting, artistic culture will perish, and that 'creative' freedom - that which reveals itself in easel painting - must not become extinct, even for an instant, otherwise it will be the end of art. We suggest that the theme of the picture is of absolutely no value, and that it is an abstract and 'free' game of pictorial shapes. But for easel painters this is not important! What is important for them is the 'atemporal', 'extra-usefulness' and 'purely aesthetic' value of their work, which it is possible to gaze and regaze at and to feel a part of; it is this that will save artistic culture. This is how monks reason. Their life, according to the outside world saves, the world. All easel painters are in agreement. If it is ever possible to save painting, then it is only in this way. If it is true that easel painting is indispensable to the existence of an artistic culture, and that without it, artistic culture is destined to perish, then it follows that it is essential to exercise all necessary measures for its development and its blossoming. But it is not true. Easel painting is not only useless to our contemporary artistic culture, but it also directly constitutes a strong brake to its development. Why is this? Naturally the worst evil is not in the monastic judgments of the 'purists' of easel painting. They easily break down in the light of anti-religious and anti-aesthetic propaganda. The evil is instead that these monastic dogmas turn into production and pedagogical principles. The fact is that easel painters do not deny the importance and necessity of other forms of artistic culture. They tolerate, without doubt, the existence of propaganda posters, designs for fine printed cotton and book covers; the only trouble is that they insist on saying that without easel painting all these 'minor' art forms are inconceivable, and that easel painting is the creative base upon which one must build every pictorial culture. This implies that, if one wants to make a beautiful printed cotton, one needs to learn how to paint landscapes. Easel painters say that the artist, no matter where he works and whatever he makes, must be a master of artistic culture and must have an artistic education, and that he obtains that culture and artistic education from easel painting. In unraveling the 'secrets' of easel painting, the artist discovers the 'secrets' of every pictorial activity, whether it be indienne, book covers, posters or theatrical decorations. And in that point of view easel painters are grossly mistaken. The picture is the product of a specific form of artistic work. Making a picture requires learning a certain number of techniques and a certain measure of ability, and it is precisely those special techniques and that certain ability that are necessary to make a picture. But from that how does one uphold the opinion that technique and ability are universal? How can one demonstrate that the technique and the ability necessary for one kind of art are necessary for all arts? Let's admit, if you like, that there are possible coincidences and that some of the techniques are general. But why then is a certain art fundamental with regards to another? Why does painting a still life have to be more important than producing a lightweight printed cotton? Why should one ever need to firstly learn how to paint still life before producing indienne, and not vice versa? Easel painters like to compare the 'pure' art of easel painting with pure mathematics. They say that one as much as the other draws on the principles and general propositions that are then put into practice. Easel painters forget that painting is not a science, that above all it is a practice and that no general proposition can be defined. The practice of the easel painter is not the practice of the painter in general, but only the practice of a particular form of artistic activity. Easel painters want to reaffirm their right to exist. If easel painting is dead as a socially necessary form of art, it can now come back to life as a universal method and as a superior school of every artistic practice. This is the way in which conscientious defenders of the necessity of the study of Ancient Classical Greek and Latin in secondary school have clinched their argument. Above all the educational universality of easel painting is refuted not only by critical theory but also by daily experimentation. The sad destiny of artists who are supposed to be experienced in easel painting and who have now tried to apply their knowledge and ability to production is noted: the result is dreadful. But, for the easel painter who instead shows no interest in production the phrase production art flows easily from his lips. However, for easel painters, production work will always be second rate and it is for this reason that they never discover methods of doing such work and thus the solution to the problems of production art will never come from them. Only those artists who, once and for all break away from easel painting, and who recognize that production art, is not only on an equal footing with artistic work, but is the only way possible, can productively and successfully resolve the problems of the current artistic culture. To this group of artists, for now not very big, need to be added the members of the INChUK: Rodchenko, Lavinsky, Vesnin, Stepanova, Ioganson, Senkin, Klutsis and Liubov Popova as well as a few less well-known ones. There is a very serious objection that easel painters make to the productivists. They say to them: 'Your work is nothing more than primitive applied art; you produce exactly what artists of applied art produce, that is, easel designs 'applied' to factory produced objects. What would you do if there was no easel painting? What would you apply to these objects?' In effect artistic work and factory work are still divided. The artist is still a stranger in the factory. He encounters suspicion there, and can not get too near. He is not believed. He does not manage to understand the technical processes which it is necessary to know about, even though he wants to know about pure industry. His work is to design and paint, while the work of the factory is to apply and stick these designs onto objects already produced. One of the main points about production art, and how an object looks, is that it is determined by its economic destination and not by abstract or aesthetic considerations, and this is still not sufficiently appreciated by our industrialists, for whom it seems, the artist wanting to go deeply into the 'economic secrets' of the object, is interfering in things which have nothing to do with him. Hence applied art is an inevitable result of the existing split between the artist and production. And this split makes the artist, who does not receive the necessary economic directives, slip willy-nilly, whether he wishes or not, towards creating esoteric designs. What consequences need to be overcome? Firstly, to overcome this split! Firstly, towards the union of the artist with the factory! And never to turn back towards pure applied art, or pictures. The artists of the Avantgarde are already walking away from the picture towards the fine printed cotton, naturally, they will not return. But this is not yet enough. The whole mass of artistic youth should understand that this march is the only way forward, and that it really needs, through this march, to develop artistic culture. It is necessary that our industrialists understand the importance of their role, inasmuch as the development of this historic process depends on them. The initiative of the director of the 'First Factory of Printed Cotton in Moscow' (the Zindel factory) the Archangel company, and Professor Viktorov, who invited the artists Stepanova and Popova into the factory, merit every attention and praise. And if it is still too early to talk about the results of this first experiment, one needs however to talk about its enormous cultural significance. The artistic culture of the future is produced in the factory and not in musty studios. It is good that artistic youth remember that, if they don't want to finish up before their time in the archives, with other easel painters.

O.M. Brik *Lef*, 1924, 2 (6), pp.27-34.

ORGANIZATIONAL PLAN OF THE PROGRAMME FOR A COURSE IN ARTISTIC COMPOSITION AT THE FACULTY OF TEXTILE OF THE VKhUTEMAS, 1925

V.F. Stepanova

1. Composition of designs of a preparatory nature for all sectors of the textile industry with the aim of learning the relationships between composition principles and colour.

a) compose a design in a plain form.
b) compose a design in a lined form.
c) compose a design composed of plain and lined forms.
d) design reproducible graphics (of a grilled type).
e) compose a design with a distinct and well spaced out structure.
f) demonstrate the use of a colour for a monochromatic design; the same exercise for designs of two or more colours.
g) design a colour combination that changes completely the compositional character of a given model.
h) reduce and/or multiply the elements of a design in order to find the fundamental proportions of the shapes of a given composition.
i) design a colour combination according to the principle of the chromatic complementarity in order to create the effect of a third colour.
l) plan a bichromatic design in order to create a multi-coloured effect.
m) compose a design which creates chromatic effects (for example, iridescence).
   The themes of the exercises up until l) include projects for printed materials and textiles as well as for designs for single parts of a garment and finished articles.

2. Design samples for the textile industry for use in the production of finished articles

a) in one colour only.
Exercises: trimmings for covers, towels, gloves and table linen.
b) in two colours.
Exercises: scarves and handkerchiefs, football socks (reinforced and knitted designs), shoes, knitted hats and belts etc.
c) in more than two colours.
Exercises: sports vests, shawls, flags, knitted clothes, curtains, carpets, etc.

3. Production and creativity in the textile industry.

A. COMPOSITION OF A DESIGN FOR A FABRIC FOR PERSONAL USE

a) lightweight fabrics 1 - with a design sketch 2 - choice of colour for a fabric without a design sketch.
Exercises: voile, printed cotton, interwoven cotton, light woolen fabric, realization of a complete outfit in its different parts, linen, etc.
b) heavy fabrics 1 - with a design sketch 2 - choice of colour for a fabric without a design sketch 3 - treatment of the fabric (sewing) 4 - choice of various fabrics and their combination with different materials.
Exercises: fabric for skirts, covers, trousers, fabrics for heavy clothes.

B. COMPOSITION OF DESIGNS FOR FABRICS FOR PUBLIC USE

Exercises: sample fabrics and designs for furnishing, drapes, curtains, chair covers, table and hotel linen.

4. Designs for fabrics and clothing.

a) work clothes.
Exercises: machinists, mechanics, workers, weavers, printers, switchboard operators, drivers, agronomists, etc.
b) protective clothing.
Exercises: health personnel, firemen, etc.
c) sportswear.
Exercises: kit for basket-ball, hockey and football teams as well as for gym clubs, track-suits for physical exercise and every other sport.
d) uniforms.
Exercises: employees of individual firms and businesses or otherwise (ticket collectors, office workers, staff of the *Moselprom*, etc.), schoolchildren and students (orphanages, schools, higher institutions).
e) everyday wear.
Exercises: clothes for parties, recurring events, public demonstrations and processions, indoor clothes, clothes for all uses, underwear, etc.
f) theatrical costume.

The graphic plan of the fabrics and of the outfit includes: a realistic and practical outfit, shoes, hats etc. The choice of the material for the outfit is based on four designs:

1 - fabric with a design sketch.
2 - choice of coloured fabrics.
3 - combination of fabrics in one shade and designed fabrics.
4 - combination of different materials suitable for the job: leather, oilskin, cloth, etc.

5. Designs for emblems, banners and flags, costume embroidery, details of clothing, shop windows.

Exercises: flags and emblems for the 'Dobrochim' (Voluntary Association for the Chemical Industry), the 'Dobrolet' (Voluntary Association for the Air Industry), for amateur radio operators, postmen's caps, insignia for military units, belts, ladies capes, lapels, etc.

6. Study research on the development and the establishment of a modern style.

a) direct observation and fashionable design sketches for fabrics produced by Soviet industry.
b) study of the evolution and changes in the said 'fashion' and relative analysis.
c) study of today's reality, with the aim of developing methods which demonstrate the awareness of the commands which new social conditions impose.

The schedule refers to a four-year course; the first year does not include the study of point 3, which starts at the end of the second year. The third year does not include point 1. With the exception of the above-mentioned differences, every year of the course always includes exercises of major complexity and pays great attention to detail.

L.G.

HOW ARE WE GOING TO DRESS?
A DISCUSSION:
EXPRESSING YOUR OPINION AT
THE RIGHT TIME

'Jungsturm'.

The sewing workshops, both private and cooperative, are not able to satisfy the orders for the 'Jungsturm' uniform, for men or for women, that flood in from all sectors. This is surprising and is also proof that there is a real opportunity for improving the clothing of our young, and that there is a clearly expressed need for a style of clothing which is both 'ours', Soviet and Komsomol, and which contrasts with the 'haute couture' designs in the shops on the Petrovka and Kuzneckij Most. From this, above all, emerges a whole series of problems: is it really fashion which is needed, is it a fashion of beauty? Will it find a place in the system of formative and cultural activity of our Komsomol? No, it is definitely not beautiful. The monotonous khaki colour of the skirts, the short trousers and the shirts, the cut of the men's shirts and the skirts, their caps and hair styles - none of these is particularly attractive, mainly because they are in fact what is needed. In every case it is quite improbable that the uniform, in its present state, can become an accepted way of dressing either for our young or for the workers and peasantry. There is a threat that it could become a barrier which divides the Komsomol, if not the superior classes then those who dress a little better than the rest of the masses. Also the 'new look' will quite quickly become antiquated. Nevertheless the very fact that it has appeared must make us reflect on a rather serious problem: we must create a true Soviet 'fashion' of our very own. We are advisedly trying to get the better of the imitators of the dandy dressers of Petrovka, with their famous foreign creations. We are trying to create new styles of hygienic clothing, practical throughout, aesthetically pleasing and made from materials of the highest quality as well as new styles which will be a general guide for all our young. We will reunite, boys and girls of the Komsomol who go to cutting and sewing classes, those who work permanently in textiles, textile designers, and the like, and we will organize fashion shows for the 'new fashion'; we will create 'cadres' who will spread the new style during public holidays, in various clubs and holiday resorts and just like in the West, the latest creations of the best tailors and dressmakers will be exhibited at the races, balls and at the opera. To sum up, we must try systematically on a technical and scientific basis, to satisfy the demands for a new style of dressing which is emerging from the fashion 'Jungsturm'.

Published in *Komsomolskaya Pravda* on 30 June 1928.

AN INTRODUCTION TO THE FIRST SOVIET EXHIBITION OF NATIONAL TEXTILES, MOSCOW, 1928

A. Fedorov-Davydov

The cultural revolution clearly demonstrated the urgency for an amalgamation between art and artistic forms for the masses, particularly in the design of household furnishings and goods for everyday use. Without denying the vitality and importance that fine arts (painting and sculpture) have today, nobody can claim that at this moment in time these art forms lend themselves to mass production or are strongly mechanized, as are posters and postcards (let's leave easel painting out of it) which can achieve wide distribution and maintain a continual and constant presence in the minds of the population, who are entitled to have artistic elements in furnishings, clothing, ceramics and the like. It is not a question of pure numerical superiority in time and space. The fact is that sculpture and painting, on the one hand, and art applied to the design of objects for daily use on the other, fulfil different functions.

A painting or sculpture is an emotional entity based on the interaction of images, which is more or less enjoyable in a direct and clear way. It is always logically assessed and understood by the human eye, within its confines which are those of figurative art. The design of objects for everyday use however, (their form, colour and decoration), directly revives our emotions, often going completely beyond every logical association. This purely automatic perception is reflected in the deeper levels of the mind and in the social behaviour of the individual.

Among the diverse applied arts, textile design is one of the most important. As a kind of primary necessity, millions of metres of fabric are produced annually in our country and find their way into even the most remote areas, populated more by bears than anything else, and into the houses of the most backward of people. As one of the primary necessities, marketable in the city and in the countryside, textiles were among the first things from the new culture to reach the most solitary and far flung regions. Machine made fabrics tended to overshadow home made materials which as a rule were created, thanks to the servile or semi-servile work of women, and thus they introduced an element of change into the closed circle of subsistence, and cleared the way for industrialization and a progressive urban culture. From this it is clear that textile design is entitled to play an enormous part in transforming old tastes and breaking old aesthetic habits and traditions (together with the ideological rules so deeply rooted in them) and it is a vehicle for a new culture and a new ideology. It responds, even if in a slightly unusual way, to the use of textile products in an urban environment and to the role they play in the organization of a new ideology in the minds of the proletariat and working masses.

The potential significance of textile products as propaganda factors has for some time been studied in depth, as is vouched for by N. N. Sobolev's article in the 'History of Textile Design'. Consequently only an extremely naive and primitive person would consider textiles simply as carriers of printed designs, a practice that unfortunately continues up until today in our country. As new methods and elements are adopted, the fundamentals themselves of design are misunderstood. All this has resulted, partly from the anomalous position of art inside a capitalist society, where it is sub-divided into different types of practical activity, and partly from a mistaken comprehension about the aims of mass art, which either ignores or actually despises the problem of raising the culture level of the masses. Similar tendencies are also recognizable in other sectors of artistic industrial production, and constitute the legacy of past traditions, which have still not been eliminated.

In a capitalist society, where in the final analysis, production is regulated by competing market forces, and where the only aim is to obtain the maximum profit possible, the artistic aspect of textile production is no more than an economic question. Textile design is used simply to attract the consumer and quite often it serves only to mask the bad quality of the fabrics themselves.

Textile products, subject to fashion changes, are however conceived like fashion itself, with the aim of satisfying the demand that the competition imposes and the need to grab the largest slice of the market possible; at the same time they play a specific class role. Expensive clothes and the latest fashions indicate that whoever is wearing them is distinguished and well-to-do, and this creates an aesthetic barrier between different classes in society. All that promotes, not only a rapid change in fashion, but also a rapid succession of cheap copies of every new product: a vulgar pandering to bourgeois taste, encapsulated in the barbarous impoverishment of cheap mass production. Textile production in pre-revolutionary Russia was just this: an ugly copy of the Western model and a result of the backward and provincial character of Russian capitalism. As Sobolev rightly demonstrated, the designs and colours of Russian fabrics were almost always copied from French originals.

'Paris' material for the city dwellers, cheap printed textiles with '*lubok*' motifs and grey calico for the countryside, and lively coloured designs and coarse, shoddy materials for the trade in the East (for example the famous design, 'pendulum', roses as big as fists and every sort of imitation of Western textiles) - this was the sum total of the artistic content of our pre-revolutionary textile industry.

Obviously, there was no possibility whatsoever of developing an indigenous artistic tradition, even if at that time materials influenced consumers at all social levels; what is more, their Western prototypes represented clear aesthetic values belonging to a given class. Wanting to mistakenly correct the textile product at that stage of its development, by giving it some sort of political or ideological significance, or wanting to see it not simply as 'good' but as 'good ideologically', would have seemed rather strange, if not downright ridiculous.

For these reasons it is not surprising that the textile industry, one of the most important light industries in the old Russia, did not create any cultural tradition worthy of mentioning, during the many years of its pre-revolutionary existence. The successes which were achieved during the transient years of the Revolution were also insignificant, both from the point of view of quality and even more so, of quantity. Our tendency was still that of slavishly following the West both in the style of the design and in continuing to follow the old Russian example of insignificant variation.

As well as the lack of a serious aesthetic tradition, an ulterior and grave obstacle to the development, in the artistic sense, of the textile industry, is constituted by the continual incumbent shortage of consumer goods, with a demand that far exceeds what is being supplied. Not only do we totally lack the incentive to compete, but the consumers themselves do not have any way of influencing the producers or of making their own tastes known to them. Moreover, those who are entrusted with the progress of the economy, in particular the representatives of commercial organizations, show themselves to be particularly conservative with regards to textile design and are not in fact inclined to encourage innovation or experimentation which goes against a taste dictated by old habits and traditions.

The scarcity of goods is certainly temporary, a transitory phenomenon, which will be overcome by wide industrial development. When that happens, industry will be more or less obliged to curry favour with the consumer and to follow his tastes. Above all, given the great political and cultural significance of textile art, we can not leave it to the mercy of market forces nor can we consider it as a purely economic or organizational problem. It is essential that we bring the discussion to the attention of public opinion and stimulate the interest of the masses, encouraging them to understand and to use their active influence on the art of textile design. For the producers and retailers on the one hand it is useful, even indispensable, that they can show to the public their work and what they have produced and acquired in the transient years of the Revolution. It is extremely important and educational that we have the opportunity of making visual and tangible contact, of seeing if the goods produced in our factories correspond to the established standard of State commerce and the cooperatives. Likewise we must see to it that the achievements and the control mechanisms instituted by various organizations, are an adequate effective response to the real demand which exists at a local level.

This show is only a small step towards the aims of those who are involved. Up until today textile design appeared only in 'decorative art' exhibitions (for example in Moscow in 1923 and 1925 at the International Paris Exhibition and in 1924 at the Exposition of Arts and People of the USSR). Such exhibitions only show the best results and rare pieces which are specifically created for the exhibition occasion and as such, they obviously prevail even over the work of fine craftsmen. However, they are precious objects which never, or almost never, appear in our daily life and have very little in common with the world of standardized textile production. From the aesthetic point of view, the trend favours traditional themes which exaggerate the so called 'popular art' and 'local colour', particularly when the exhibition is held abroad.

This exhibition of national Soviet textiles has instead been created with all together different motives and shows a completely different type of fabric. Organized on the inspiration of the Society of Weaver Artists, the show intends to present the actual state of the textile industry as a whole, as much industrial production as artisanal. Mass produced textiles and those used in everyday clothing in the city and the country are exhibited. Our aim is not to gain publicity or to show something off, even in the most innocent way, but rather to offer an overall vision not only of our successes but of our mistakes, our bad points, our traditions and a certain experience. All this is in harmony with the vital forces of revolutionary thought which recall a realistic picture of our current situation and which demonstrate both the tendencies and the sense of direction of latest developments. It is not an exhibition of decorative arts, but of art in industry based on practical considerations and suitability rather than on abstract aesthetic ideals.

The exhibition deals with the widest range of yarns and the largest possible forms of design (clothing, Jacquards, printed textiles, dying techniques, embroidery, etc.). Alongside manufactured examples, a section is dedicated to the creations of students and designers working with industry. For the purposes of comparison the works shown by productive organizations are, where possible, placed side by side with works from the pre- revolutionary period.

Naturally such a show is a long way from being complete and its organizers are the first to recognize this. Their only hope is that visitors manage to appreciate the trouble they went to in organizing such an innovative project. This is the first exhibition of textile design and that in itself is already enough to confer upon it an exceptional significance, despite all its defects and errors, some of which were absolutely inevitable.

L.G.

THE HISTORY OF TEXTILE DESIGN

N. Sobolev

At the end of the XIVth century it is possible to ascertain - through the changes in textile design - the taste of the dominant classes in Italy, which serves as a guide to European textile production up until the XIXth century, when Italy was overtaken by France. Magnificent Italian and French materials, embroidered and interwoven with silk and gold threads were used in Russia for clothes, drapes and furnishings. In those days there did not exist a really reliable way of printing cloth and designs were copied or adapted from these textiles.

Unfortunately, we do not possess in our collections, any printed fabric of foreign production of the XVIth, XVIIth or XVIII centuries, but studies conducted on numerous and well preserved Russian textiles from that period reveal that, apart from a few absolutely original and independent designs, they reflect various influences, both Western and Eastern. The designs of these printed textiles are a version, even if distorted, of the most expensive materials used by the ruling, secular and religious classes.

Since we know that progress in printing techniques was at the same stage of development in Russia as it was in Western Europe, we can presume that in the West the printed design had at that time an identical place of origin. It is difficult to imagine, for example, that in eighteenth century France specific fabric designs were created for use by peasants. But in all French rural pictures of that time, the peasant's clothes did not show any indication of print. In the second half of the XVIIIth century when Louis XVI abolished restrictions on the craft guilds and the printed textile officially acquired its own 'droits de citoyen' (up until then it had been prohibited by the fear of Colbert of all that could threaten the French silk factories), models of silk clothes worn by the 'third estate' began to be copied.

Until these innovations, printed materials, produced illegally, had been only copies of the more common printed designs of imported textiles, like 'Siam' or 'India', which showed - a sort of struggle between wild beasts and tropical birds - assymetrical entanglements of fantastic and enormous flowers. These designs had enormous success. They were partly printed and partly painted or coloured by specialist artists in material design.

The first designs deliberately created for cotton material and, for the first time, directly aimed at propaganda and the promotion of particular ideas, were created in France by Christophore Oberkampf, of Bavarian origin. Oberkampf, born in the Kingdom of Bavaria, spent almost all his life in France, took French citizenship and died in the small town of Jouy en Josas near Versailles, where in 1815 he had begun his work. It was his idea to produce designs of a political nature, which threw light on particular events for the semi-literate and at the same time focused attention on them. His enormous energy was sustained only by force of will and by his thirst for knowledge. It was he who laid the foundations for the printed textile industry in France using French linens rather than imported cotton from England.

Starting out with a capital of 600 francs (the equivalent of about 10 pounds then), in the early years he himself created the designs and the printing screens as well as selling the finished product. Once the productive process was perfected and mechanized after many years of experiments screen plates were gradually replaced by cylindrical plates. This idea of printing revolutionized the industry. Production increased considerably with decisively lower costs and 'linen from Jouy', as Oberkampf's materials were called, became available to almost everybody. On furnishing fabrics were represented scenes of the production at 'Jouy', from the harvest of the flax through to the cutting of the printed product, the flight of the first air-balloon of Montgolfier and many other important events of the era. Revolutionary scenes with the First Consul and the Emperor alternated with country scenes of Italy and Egypt.

The success of Oberkampf generated a considerable number of imitations. Almost all the textile factories and workshops in France, Switzerland, Germany and other nations began to work in the same way. The romantic era which dominated Europe in the years following the death of Oberkampf, were his reflection in textiles, of literary works of the period, with Calabrian brigands, very fashionable then, ruins of the classical world, Medieval castles and the like.

Identical influences can be found in the Russian printed textiles. The inauguration in Red Square, after the war of 1812, of a monument dedicated to the heroes of the seventeenth century Russia, Minin and Pozarsky, became a recurrent theme in printed textiles, with different versions of the historical subject. The fantastic world of exotic flowers, animals and birds that the Jouy materials had adapted from the designs 'Siam' and 'India' still made a great impression on the imaginations of the Russian designers: printed calico with scenes of this type were used for screens, drapery and the household furnishings of landowners and merchants.

Designs for country dwellers were made in villages by specialized artisans. Their small designs, in yellow, white and blue, on a background of dark indigo were very widespread towards the middle of the nineteenth century. Ivanovo-Voznesensk now became a flourishing centre of the textile industry, having previously been little more than a village, simply called Ivanovo, one of the feuds of the Seremet'ev family. Its population was essentially made up of artisans-designers; after the liberation of serfs in 1861, some of these artisans, the more gifted in initiative and those particularly appreciative of their art, founded a few textile factories destined to grow and acquire importance. The designs for prints created by them were the results of work done by local artists, otherwise they were copied from foreign material samples which they had had the opportunity of seeing, or were adapted from other manufacturer's models.

As well as different materials for sale by the metre, the Russian textile factories produced single pieces, above all shawls, scarves and handkerchiefs. The first shawl, which became quite famous in Europe, was the marvellous Indian shawl brought back to Josephine by Napoleon Bonaparte on his return from the Egyptian campaign. The instantaneous enthusiasm for Indian shawls meant that they were first of all copied in France and then in Germany. It was really from here, across Saxony, that they reached the Russian factories, where they immediately became famous under the name 'Saxony'. They made their appearance in the villages between 1870 and 1880, during which time the demand for them grew enormously. Besides shawls in printed cotton, wool shawls and scarfs printed in lively colours, of the type initially created in Pavlov Posad and later well-known by the name 'Old Pavlov' were just as popular. Their designs of gaily coloured flowers on a coloured background were reminiscent of Spanish shawls and their principal fascination was due to the intense aniline dyes.

The rich choice of designs for mechanized prints, which today we have at our disposition, dates back to not more than thirty or forty years ago. Before then a small number of designs existed. For the 'oriental' taste there were imitations of designs in crimson tints on a bright red background; for the countryside and the Ukraine, imitations of the old hand printed textiles in an indigo colour were produced, as well as the aforementioned 'Saxony' shawls and the 'German' scarves, with big stylized flowers on a contrasting yellow background as well as on grey calico.

With a few exceptions, the Russian factories printing textiles did not produce anything new. The prints of the Russian designers totally depended on Paris fashion and effectively the textile production of the whole world followed the orientation of Paris up until the First World War. In Paris there existed genuine workshops for the creation of textile designs, that made use of their structure to present annually the collections produced by the major French factories, and which took orders from all over the world. The Russian industry made wide use of French designs, managing at times to have French or Alsatian designers direct their design departments. The Russian artists of the time considered it rather undignified to work in the manufacturing industry and the widespread 'ideas of importance' continued up until the outbreak of the First World War, thus until 1914 there was almost no totally 'Russian' industry.

It is perfectly understandable that the foreign artists, who found themselves directing the design departments, followed their own inclinations and teachings received during their studies in Paris and, consequently, there could not exist in any sense something worthy of being called 'a typical Russian style' in the printed textiles of that era. The only difference between Russian materials and those not Russian, seen in the sections dedicated to textiles in the great international exhibitions, was the imperial insignia at the front.

For all these reasons, our textile industry, despite its long history, with the exception of a few articles created for special occasions, did not succeed until today in creating its own style. It is our era, in which we are creating a new type of life in the Soviet Republic, which urges us to that new style.

Published in the catalogue of the *First Exhibition of Russian National Textiles*, in 1928.

L.G.

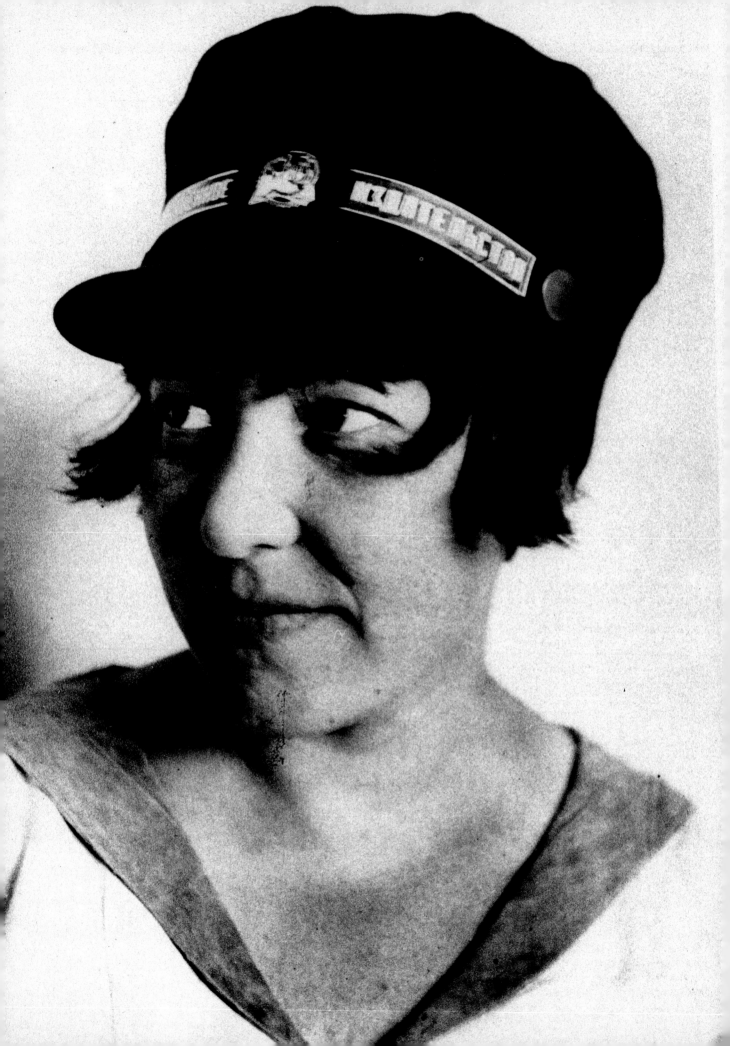

BIOGRAPHIES

Nikolai Akimov (1901-1968)
Born in Kharkov, he attended evening courses in design at the school of the Association for the Promotion of Art, in Petrograd (1914). From 1915-1916 he was a pupil of S. Zajdelberg, attending at the same time the 'New Art Studio', in Dobuzinsky's classes). From 1922 to 1924 he attended the Vkhutein in Petrograd. In 1921 he started to exhibit his work and to work in the theatre as a scenographer and later on as a producer.

Marya Anufrieva
Born in 1902 in Moscow. In 1930 she completed her studies at the Faculty of Textiles of the Vkhutein in Moscow. She worked for the manufacturer *Trechgornaya* and then for the 'First Factory of Printed Cotton'. She is the creator of innumerable works on the theme of the Revolution.

Olga Bogoslovskaya
Born in 1905 in Totma, in 1929 she finished studying at the Mstera Art School, in the province of Ivanovo. She worked as a textile designer in the factory *Krasnaya Talka* (Red Spinning-Mill) and from 1931 to 1933 at the 'United Manufacturers *Sosnev*'. She participated in numerous exhibitions in the USSR and abroad.

Sarra Buncis
Born in 1903 in Odessa, from 1924 to 1928 she studied at the Kiev Art School in Meller's class and in 1930 at the Textile Institute in Moscow. Since 1930 she has been a designer in the 'V. Sluckaya' factory and in the 'A. Zeljabov' dye-works . She taught for a long while at the 'V. Mukhina' Higher School of Industrial Design in Leningrad.

Sergej Burylin (1876-1942)
Born in Ivanovo-Voznesensk, son of an engraver, he started work at the 'Great Manufacturer Ivanovo-Voznesensk' and later on – up until the Thirties – in the '*Ziderev*' factory, again at Ivanovo. Sergei Burylin – one of the major talented textile designers of the Twenties – took part in numerous exhibitions in the USSR and abroad, including that of the Decorative Arts in Paris, in 1925.

Michail Chvostenko (1902-1976)
Studied at the Faculty of Painting at the Vkhutein from 1925 to 1930. He is the creator of many design themes and, from the beginning of the Thirties, of floral designs for textiles produced by the '*Trechgornaya*' factories in Moscow. In the Fifties and Sixties he taught at the Textile Institute in Moscow.

Alexandra Exter (1882-1949)
Born in 1882 in Belostok near Kiev, she studied at the Kiev Art School. In 1908 she went to Paris to attend the Chaumiére Academy, where she made friends with Picasso, Braque, Appollinaire and Jacob. In the years 1909-1914 she lived in Kiev, Moscow and Paris, where she knew Ardengo Soffici, with whom she visited Italy. In 1921 she started making clothes and textiles in the Constructivist style. As a scenographer and costume designer we remember Exter's extraordinary Cubo-Futurist scenery and costumes which she created for the Moscow Little Theatre (for 'Tamin the Citharodeus', 'Romeo and Juliet', 'Salome'), and the extravagant costumes for 'Aelita'. In 1924 she emigrated to France, where she created costumes for Nijinsky, Kruger and Pavlova. From 1925 she was a professor at Fernand Leger's Academy in Paris.

Oskar Grjun (1874-1931)

Finished his studies at the *'Shtiglits'* Technical Design Institute in St Petersburg in 1897, from 1899 to 1919, and then from 1922 to 1931, he was a designer for the cotton *'Trechgornaya'* factories in Moscow. He is the creator of a well-known series of design themes with which he participated in exhibitions in the USSR and abroad.

Natalya Kiseleva (1906-1951)

Born in Samara in 1906 of a country family, she moved to Moscow in 1923 in order to attend the *'Profintern'* Teaching Institute . On finishing her studies in 1927 she enrolled – in the same year – at the Vkhutein to perfect her work and then at the Moscow Textile Institute. Natalya Kiseleva was deeply influenced by Cubism and in her decorations she shows unquestionable similarites to the paintings of Alexandra Exter and to the textiles of Ludmilla Mayakovskaya. At the end of her studies Kiseleva worked for *'Krasnosvej'* (Red Sewing), designing work overalls and at the same time textiles for the *'Krasnaya Roza'* (Red Rose) factory. Towards the mid-Thirties she created stage costumes for some of the theatres in Stalingrad and created uniforms for the sports competitions in Moscow.

Alexandra Kolcova-Byckova (1892-1985)

In 1918 she completed her studies at the *'Stroganov'* Artistic-Industrial Institute and attended the Vkhutemas. She was a notable textile designer, and perfected her skills – from 1928 to 1931 – in Paris. From the mid-Thirties, she ceased to dedicate herself to textile design.

Nadezda Lamanova (1861-1941)

Born in the village of Shulizov, in the province of Nizhegorod, she studied at the *'O. Suvorovaya'* cutting-school and then in the *'Vojtkevic'* workshop. In 1885 she opened her own workshop. From 1919 she taught industrial design at the teaching division of the IZO, at the same time voluntarily directing the Workshop of Contemporary Costume. In 1921 she was elected to the Board of Directors of the Handicraft department in the Academy of Fine Arts. From 1901 she designed theatrical costume for the *'Mkhat'* Art Theatre and, from 1916, at the *'Vachtangov'*. From the Twenties she dedicated herself to the cinema, creating costumes for 'Aelita', 'Alexander Nevsky', 'Circo', 'Ivan the Terrible' and 'A Generation of Victors'. Nadezda Lamanova won the Grand Prix at the Paris Exhibition of Decorative Arts in 1925 and played a part in determining the theoretical plan of Soviet Fashion.

Vera Lotonina (b. 1910)

Born in 1910 in Pushkin, in the province of Leningrad, from 1927 to 1930 she studied at the Vkhutein and from 1930 to 1932 she studied design at the Moscow Textile Institute. In 1928 she joined the youth section of the Association of Artists of Revolutionary Russia, creating propagandist as well as everyday aesthetic design themes. From 1932 to 1935 she directed the Design Workshop of the *'Krasnaya Roza'* (Red Rose) silk-factory, creating floral designs for crepe de Chine. After having left the Red Rose she worked with textile firms in Moscow, Leningrad and Ivanovo. From 1943 she dedicated herself to the making of curtains, covers, tablecloths and above all tapestries destined for public buildings in Moscow and abroad.

Ludmilla Mayakovskaya (1884-1963)

Born in the village of Nikitinka in Armenia, she studied – from 1904 to 1910 – textile printing at the '*Stroganov*' Artistic-Industrial Institute in Moscow. In 1909 she worked at the '*Mussi*' silk-factory, where she learnt the spray-gun technique. On finishing her studies she was employed by the Design Workshop of the '*Prokhorov*' and later '*Trechgornaya*' factories, directed by Oskar Grjun. At the end of 1910 she was asked to manage the Spray-Gun Printing Workshop, a technique which the artist perfected, experimenting for a long time on silk, muslin and velvet, materials quite difficult to find in the first ten post-revolutionary years. The style of Mayakovskaya in the Twenties was inspired by Constructivist geometrics, usually on a dark background: circles, broken lines, multi-coloured surfaces which velvet made darker and variable. Some of Mayakovskaya's materials were presented at the Paris Exhibition of Decorative Arts in 1925, where they won a silver medal. For about 40 years Ludmilla Mayakovskaya was heavily involved in teaching, first of all at the Vkhutemas-Vkhutein (1921-1930) and then at the Moscow Textile Institute.

Nadezda Makarova (1898-1969)

Born in Moscow, on leaving high school, she taught in the province of Kaluga. She returned to the capital and was employed as a dressmaker in the House of Lamanova, near to where she lived. In 1923-1924 she attended the studio of the painter Juon, whilst working at the same time in the Workshop for Contemporary Costume and, from 1927, at the *Kustexport* (Agency for the Exportation of Art Objects). From the mid Twenties, Makarova worked with the Art Theatre, with the '*Vachtangov*' and the Meyerhold Theatre. In 1934 she was nominated Director of the Moscow Fashion House (1924-1939 and 1945-1949). In her work Nadezda Makarova consistently developed the line of Lamanova, an upholder of practical clothing with a simple cut, adapted to the mass buyer.

Raisa Matveeva (b. 1906)

Born in 1906, she was first of all dedicated to painting, then – from 1927 to 1930 – to textile design for the 'Great Manufacturer' in Ivanovo. She is the creator of a series of textile designs presented at numerous Soviet exhibitions.

Marya Nazarevskaya (b. 1898)

Born in 1898 in Moscow, studied design in '*Precistinkie*' courses and, from 1924 to 1929, at the Vkhutemas-Vkhutein in the Faculty of Textile Design. The creator of notable thematic designs for textiles and carpets, she took part in numerous exhibitions in the USSR and abroad.

Ljubov Popova (1889-1924)

Born in the village of Ivanovo, in the suburbs of Moscow, she attended – in the years 1907-1908 – the art studio of the painter Zhukovsky and the schools of painting and design of Juon and Dudin. In 1912-1913 she studied at the La Palette Academy in Paris and from 1913 to 1915 she worked on the *Tower*, with the artist Tatlin. In 1918 she became a Board member of the IZO and, from 1920 a member of the Inkhuk. In 1921 she started to learn textile design at the Vkhutemas. In the years 1923-1924 she was employed by the design workshop of the 'First Factory of Printed Cotton' in Moscow, creating new types of geometric decoration. As a scenographer and costume designer we remember Popova's famous Constructivist production of 'The Magnanimous Cuckold' for the Meyerhold theatre.

Darya Preobrazenskaya (1908-1972)

After having studied at the Faculty of Textile Design at the Vkhutemas-Vkhutein, she found employment as a textile designer in the 'Great Manufacturer' of Ivanovo (1929-1931) and, then with the '*Trechgornaya*' factory in Moscow. Her works have been exhibited many times in the USSR.

Lya Rajcer (b. 1902)

Born in 1902 into a worker's family, he started work – in the civil war years – in the sewing workshops of the Red Army. From 1919 to 1920 he attended the Institute of Applied Art in Perm, from where he transferred to Moscow in order to enroll at the Vkhutemas, where he finished in 1930. In 1928 he founded and directed the youth section of the Association of Artists of Revolutionary Russia, in which he learnt to propagandize the rejection of every aesthetic embellishment. Rajcer was, in fact, one of the first to design material – for clothes and furnishing – and to use themes linked to the Revolution.

Alexander Rodchenko (1891-1956)

Born in Petrograd, he studied at the Kazan Art School with N. Fesin and, from 1914 to 1916, at the '*Stroganov*'

Artistic-Industrial Institute in Moscow. In the Twenties he was in charge of the Metallurgical Faculty first of the Vkhutemas and then of the Vkhutein. In 1920 he was elected to the Board and in 1921 he was president of the Inkhuk. He designed decor and costumes for many performances at the Meyerhold Theatre, made work clothes, furniture and other types of small-scale architecture. In the beginning of the Thirties he dedicated himself to photography, posters, collages, industrial graphics, books and magazines. He took part in numerous exhibitions in the USSR and abroad. In 1925, at the Paris Exhibition of Decorative Arts, he was awarded four silver medals.

Ljubov Silic (b. 1906)

Born in 1906, she studied at the Faculty of Textile Design of the Vkhutemas-Vkhutein. She is the creator of notable thematic decorations for textiles.

Varvara Stepanova (1894-1958)

Born in Kovno, she studied at the Kazan Art School and, then at the studios of Juon and Dudin in Moscow. In 1918 she was elected to the Board of the IZO and, in 1920, she became a member of the Inkhuk. In the years 1924 to 1925 she taught at the Faculty of Textile Design at the Vkhutemas, working at the same time with Popova in the design workshop of the 'First Factory of Printed Cotton' in Moscow, where she created new types of geometric designs. She made costumes and scenes, in 1922, for the famous comedy-farce 'The Death of Tarelkin', and designed – often in collaboration with her husband – books, periodicals and albums. In the years 1945-1946 she worked on the magazine *Soviet*

Woman. She took part in numerous exhibitions in the USSR and abroad.

Vladimir and Georgy Sternberg: Vladimir (1899-1983) Georgy (1900-1933)

Born in Moscow, they studied – from 1912 to 1917 – at the '*Stroganov*' Institute in Moscow and, in 1920 at the Vkhutemas. They were amoung the more enlightened supporters of the Constructivist movement which fully developed within the Inkhuk. From 1924 to 1931 they created scenery and costumes for the Chamber Theatre, bringing themselves to the attention of the more faithful collaborators of Alexander Tairov. The Sternberg brothers were typically representative of Constructivist scenographers, active – in particular Vladimir – in urban context design.

Vladimir Tatlin (1895-1953)

Born in Moscow, he studied at the Painting, Sculpture and Architecture Institute (1902-1903, 1909-1910) – in Serov and Korovin's classes – and at the Penza Art School (1904-1909). He taught at the Vkhutemas and at the Vkhutein, at the Petrograd Art Academy (1921-1927) and at the Kiev Art Institute (1925-1927). From 1918 to 1921 he managed the IZO in Moscow. In 1912 he joined 'Painting Infantry' following Cubism and Futurism in order to become, in the end, one of the major theorists of Constructivist production. His project for a Monument to the Third International (the *Tower*, 1919-1920) and the *Le tatlin ornithopter* (1930-1931) were major and memorable works. His theatrical activity is of great interest with scenery and costumes for 'King Maximilian and Zangese' of Khlebnikov. From 1917, the year in which with Rodchenko and Jakulov he planned the furnishing for the 'Café pittoresque' in Moscow, he applied himself to design.

GLOSSARY

General terms
GINKHUK

(*Gosudarstvennyj institut khudozest-vennoj kultury*). State Institute of Artistic Culture. Founded in Petrograd in 1923 and based on the example of the Muscovite INKHUK. Punin, the left-wing critic was elected scientific secretary of the Council, made up of Malevich, Tatlin, Filonov, Matjusin and Mansurov. It was disbanded in 1926.

INKHUK

(*Institut khudozestvennoj kultury*) Institute of Artistic Culture. Set up in 1920, by the IZO of the NARKOMPROS. It was presided over firstly by Kandinsky, who developed its programme, then by Rodchenko; the secretaries of production were Tarabukin and Stepanova. The Constructivist group were formed here in 1921 and were led by Rodchenko, Stepanova and Gan. The Institute, where, for the first time, theoretical and aesthetic principles of Soviet design were formed, was disbanded in 1924.

IZO

(*Otdel izobrazitelnych iskusstv*) Department of Fine Arts. Founded in 1918 by the NARKOMPROS. It was the appointed body for the management of cultural politics in the visual arts sector and was directed by Tatlin until 1921 (Muscovite section) and by Sternberg (Petrograd section).

NARKOMPROS

(*Narodnyj komissariat po prosvescen-iju*) People's Commissariat of Enlightenment. Founded in 1917 by the People's Council of Delegates who controlled the state administration, it was led by Lunacharsky until 1929. This body co-ordinated the management of general cultural and educational policy. In 1936 the two functions were separated. The Commissariat was disbanded in 1949 and transformed into Ministries.

VKHUTEMAS

(*Vyscie khudozestvenno-tekhiceskie masterskie*) Higher State Artistic-Technical Studios founded in 1920 on the ashes of the dissolved 'Free Art Studios' I and II and included an artistic faculty (painting, sculpture and architecture) and one for industrial production (design, weaving, ceramics, woodwork and metalwork) the latter modelled on the systems of the Bauhaus. The manifesto of the Artistic Council, read at the inauguration, stated that the aim of the new Institute was 'To bring art and industry closer together and to develop in the worker the precepts of the artist'. Rodchenko ran, from 1921 to 1924, the Metallurgical Faculty and Stepanova taught weaving from 1924 to 1925. Among the teachers in the Constructivist wing we should mention Tatlin and El Lissitsky (woodwork and metalwork), Udalcova and Drevin (painting), Klucis (theory of colour) and Ladovsky (architecture) as well as Exter, Popova and Mayakovskaya (textile design). The Institute was disbanded in 1926.

VKHUTEIN

(*Vyscij khudozestvenno-tekhniceskij institut*) Higher State Technical Institute. The Leningrad institute, modelled on the Vkhutemas, was founded in 1922 and closed in 1930. Most of the teachers were from the GINKHUK. The Muscovite institute was founded in 1926 and even though it inherited the ideology and reassembled the dissolved programmes of the VKHUTEMAS, from where it also recruited the teaching body, it slipped rapidly towards a marked return to traditional pre-Revolutionary teaching principles, giving preference to easel painting which was one of the main targets of the Constructivist and Productionist avant-garde. It was closed in 1930.